Stale Bread?

Stale Bread?

A Handbook for Speaking the Story

RICHARD LITTLEDALE

SAINT ANDREW PRESS
EDINBURGH

*To Fiona, Joseph, Jonathan and Luke, whose stories
are bound up with mine, and whose encouragement
allowed this story to be written.*

First published in 2007 by
SAINT ANDREW PRESS
121 George Street, Edinburgh EH2 4YN

ISBN 978 0 7152 0835 9

British Library Cataloguing in Publication Data
A catalogue record for this book is available from the British Library

It is the Publisher's policy to only use papers that are natural and recyclable and that have
been manufactured from timber grown in renewable, properly managed forests. All of
the manufacturing processes of the papers are expected to conform to the environmental
regulations of the country of origin.

Typeset by Waverley Typesetters, Fakenham
Printed and bound by Bell & Bain Ltd, Glasgow

Contents

    A stale preaching ministry is not a finished preaching ministry. An experience of preaching which has become stale, for both preachers and listeners, can still be revived.

    A review of factors creating a malaise about preaching. Some are external to the Church, some are from the Christian subculture, and some are from within the Church itself.

    In the age of snappy e-mails and snappier text messages, this is a call for a reintroduction of lyrical language in the pulpit. Such language not only conveys information but also provokes emotion and arouses passion. Furthermore, a proper concern about politically correct language should not result in a language which is prosaic and insipid.

    The birth of narrative preaching, and an explanation of how it works.

commit to an organic rather than a static model of preaching. Word and Spirit abide, but the preacher must be adaptable.

A selection of small Biblical insights, organised by character and theme, to stimulate thought for narrative preaching.

Foreword

'Stale Bread?' – what an arresting title! At first, I thought: why not 'Fresh Bread'? That, after all, is what Richard Littledale longs that we bake, and taste, in our churches, as God's living word is lovingly handled week by week. But 'Stale Bread' – what does that do for you? It made me linger over the sobering thought of what, too often, may be the reality; and hunger for something different.

That 'something different' is what Richard offers us in this book: a mouth-watering sample of the kind of nourishment that, deep down, worshippers long for week by week, and, deep down, their ministers long to offer. And the startling title is a foretaste of the mode of language that he uses in his writing and commends for our speaking: surprising, unconventional, creative.

With crisp clarity, Richard deals with the spectres which haunt the ministry of preaching today and subtly neuter the preacher's will to give of his or her imaginative best. He commends and explores three varieties of 'narrative' preaching which tap into the deep human love-affair with stories, a love-affair which God himself seems to share. He is at pains to show that true narrative preaching is much more than a string of anecdotes, but is deeply rooted in the shape and sinews of particular Biblical stories, and aims – like all true preaching – at human transformation in today's world. He is further at pains to stress that the particular patterns he describes are in no way exhaustive or exclusive. They are, rather, pointers, beckoning us to a whole mood, a whole mindset: a recognition that preaching is as much an enterprise of poetry as it is of logic.

This book is an example of a general flowering of interest in the task of finding fresh yet faithful words for hungry hearts, which crosses continents and the spectrum of church life. However, it is no mere act of bandwagon-jumping, or (to revert to the controlling metaphor) reheating of food recently served elsewhere. It has a striking originality, in three ways especially. First, it is generously illustrated with examples of his own experiments in narrative preaching, accompanied by frank, vulnerable and concise assessments of their strengths and weaknesses. Second, it recognises that no preaching 'method' can be evaluated apart from the preacher's specific context, and includes a most valuable chapter on the process of helping congregations to *hear* a 'different' type of preaching. Third, it contains appetising suggestions for the reader's own imaginative engagement with some of the wonderful stories of Scripture.

Richard is a gifted teacher and writer, and a courageous preacher whose ideas and skills have been refined not in detachment from pastoral ministry but through immersion in it. This is a sparkling gem of a book, easy on the eye, yet reflecting light from afar. I will return to it for inspiration and help when I feel that my own offerings are getting stale. I warmly commend it to you.

STEPHEN I. WRIGHT
Tutor in Biblical Studies and Practical Theology,
Spurgeon's College and Oasis UK

Introduction

Pick up a crust of bread and hold it in your hand. Its crust is a rich honey colour. Here and there are bobbles of a darker brown, where the oven's heat has caused it to bubble and sear. Bring it close and smell the aroma, taking you back to kitchens and comforting meals you have known. Turn it over now and look at the open texture of the bread itself – an intricate maze of bubbles and fibres, definitely good enough to eat. Now take a bite. Urrgh! That is where the problem starts. This is stale bread. It has been carefully mixed and the dough has risen. It has been kneaded and baked to perfection. Someone has even sliced off a morsel for you. However, it is hard and unappetising. Perhaps the best thing to do would be to throw it away.

But wait! Look again at that crust of bread. Watch with amazement as it unfurls before your eyes. It stretches out and seems to grow thinner as it moves. Its edges flap over your hand now. It is no longer thick, but paper-thin. Look carefully, and the hard edges of its crust are the edges of a sheet of paper now. The holes and bubbles of the bread have been replaced with the familiar pattern of your writing. This is your sermon, the fruit of your labours. But is it stale? Would the best thing be to throw it away?

Before you answer that question, think back to the piece of bread. Is it completely useless? When I was a child, my mother taught me that there is nothing like a hunk of stale bread for bringing life back to an old hardback book. Rubbed vigorously on the book's surface, stale bread can remove years' worth of accumulated muck and grime. Alternatively, it could be soaked in milk and combined with butter and juicy sultanas to make a delicious pudding. Soaking up the richness of the milk and butter, and the sweet flavour of the sultanas, the old bread could live again. Don't throw it out!

For every listener tempted to throw their preacher out, there is a preacher tempted to do the same with either their sermon or the calling which led them to preach it. Like the bread, it has been kneaded and worked and baked. There have been hours of labour in the making, and anxious moments in the cooking. There has been many an anxious peep through the oven door to see if anything was happening. The finished result, however, has been hard and unappetising. The congregation goes away with a gnawing hunger, and the preacher goes away wringing his or her hands like a chef who has failed to feed the guests. On the basis of my encounters with other preachers of many denominations, it is my firm belief that, for every hundred listeners who are bored with preaching, there are at least ten preachers who feel the same way.

Of course, one small book cannot hope to reverse such a trend all by itself. Rather, it may sow some hope in the hearts of preachers and listeners alike that something can be done. In the pages which follow, I begin by analysing some of the factors which make it so hard to preach in the first place. After a review of the reasons, both psychological and spiritual, why preaching still has a vital place, I look at the changing nature of the language medium out of which preaching is born, and ask whether the time has come to tell stories once again.

After that, I hope to bake some fresh bread for you. Like a developer trying to sell a new house, I shall waft its scent under your nose. In Chapters 4–6, you will find yourself plunged into a multi-sensory world of storytelling. Sights, sounds and even smells await you there. After a description of how each sort of story sermon is crafted, examples are shown and analysed. Each sermon is printed exactly as it was preached – warts and all! Its success or failure is assessed, and alternative approaches given for preaching it.

Fresh from the storytelling, we shall look in more depth at the skills necessary to select a particular preaching style for a particular context. If storytelling is for you, there are chapters on how to encourage your own narrative potential, and how to introduce your congregation to this new technique.

Before rounding off with a selection of 'narrative nuggets' to get you started, there is a call for an ongoing commitment to preacher and people learning each other's language. Preaching is an organic and ever-changing ministry. As language changes, as preachers and listeners live alongside each other, as the wonderfully disruptive Spirit of God does his work, we trust that it will go on changing until the day when it is no longer needed.

Chapter 1

Crisis, what crisis?

How many of us are tired of sermons? How many of us have listened to sermons on the Second Coming where the Lord's arrival to judge the living and the dead would have been a merciful release? How many have sat through sermons within the past month where style and application demonstrated a searing relevance … to the 1970s? Worse still, how many of us have *stood* through such a sermon?.

The experience of boredom and defeat *in* the pulpit, never mind in front of it, is a serious threat to the health of the Church. It's not that we are lacking in conviction; indeed, our call to preach and pastor is as strong as it ever was. Nor are we unwilling to put in the necessary hard work. In fact, you will often find us labouring for hours at the desk long after the hospital visits are over and the youth group has gone home. The problem is not one of willingness or commitment, or even of ability, but of fatigue. Sometimes on a Sunday, we have the uncomfortable feeling that everybody in the room, themselves included, is bored by what they hear. Of course, this was not always the case. You can still remember the times when you rushed into the pulpit keen to deliver the fresh message which God had given you. Sometimes now, though, it is a different story. Some Sundays, we want to be a master chef, serving up an appetising meal for our hungry congregation, but find only a hunk of stale bread in our hand.

So, is the sermon dead? For every preacher who listens too much to his or her own sermons, there is another who listens too much to the critics of the sermon as a form. The sermon is not dead, but the bad sermon ought to be! For those who preach them, this is worrying news indeed. If you are one of those people, then you know exactly what I mean. But why do you preach anyway? Few of us do it for the glory – and we certainly don't do it for the money. No, in the end it is a matter of call. That call may have been dramatic or gradual, spoken or simply perceived. However it came, there was a time when you felt that God wanted you to proclaim his word to others. This call was then affirmed by others within the Church. As Paul points out in Romans 10:15, the preacher must preach from a divine commission. Without such a commission, you may be a speaker or a communicator, but not a preacher. Take some time to remember that call before we proceed any further. It is yours, and no-one can take it away from you. As we look now at the reasons why God uses preachers, remember that there is a very special reason why he uses *you*.

What's so good about preaching?
Biblical precedent

The Bible is full of preachers of all shapes and sizes. Some are uneducated fishermen, and others are highly skilled scholars. Some have a style which is brutally straightforward, while others bring a poetic touch to the task. Others, whether in the words they speak or the garments they wear while speaking, seem just plain weird! Of particular interest here are those preachers who articulate the Word of God for the people of God in moments of epochal change. It is to these people that the task is given of making sense of God's deeds among his children.

Consider, first of all, Ezra and his assistants in the newly rebuilt city of Jerusalem (Nehemiah 8:1–11). All around them is the newly dressed stone on which they have laboured so hard since their unexpected return from exile. Most of these people have never lived outside Babylon, and the Word of God is an alien document, the kind of thing that their grandparents talked about wistfully as they described the old days of freedom. What is Ezra the priest to do with them? First of all, he asks the carpenters to do one more bit of construction, and erect a wooden platform in one of the city's main squares. Then he gathers all the people together and begins to read God's word to them from the platform. As the crowd listens to these strange words, Ezra's assistants are moving among them, reading the same words and explaining them. There is some doubt here as to the precise meaning of the word in Nehemiah 8:8. Some versions say they 'translated' the words, others that they 'made them clear'; and the original Hebrew says that they 'divided them up'. Whichever one we choose, it is clear that they are making the Word of God plain to those for whom it is strange. Not only this, but they are doing so at a critical moment in Israel's history. Upon the people's renewed understanding of God's word, the spiritual foundations of this great city will be built. In a moment of change, with unfamiliar sights and sounds all around them, someone needed to make sense of God's word for them.

Nothing has changed, really. In a moment of change, people still need to hear the Word of God. They still need someone to 'divide it up' for them so that it makes sense. Reflecting on the experience of preaching in the immediate aftermath of the terrorist attack on the World Trade Center in 2001, Craig Barnes, Professor of Pastoral Ministry at Pittsburgh Theological Seminary, commented that 'preachers actually live for these moments of crisis'.[1] He went on to say that 'What we do best, and better than anyone else in town, is climb behind a pulpit and speak into the fear and chaos with a sacred word'. Deep down, are you still the kind of person who wants to meet that challenge?

Before you answer that question, let's spool the Biblical tape on several centuries to another gathering in the city of Jerusalem. Many years have passed since Ezra's day, and the Jews are now a scattered people. Tens of thousands of them have flocked into the city to celebrate Pentecost, the Jewish harvest festival. They have come from many lands to the traditional celebration focused on the temple. Songs will be sung, psalms will be read, and God's goodness will be remembered. This year, however, things are different. With Jesus only just raised from the dead and ascended into heaven, an ancient promise is being fulfilled before their very eyes. Although they don't know it yet, the Holy Spirit, foreseen by the ancient prophets and promised by Jesus, is falling on his followers. Bizarre things are happening, with tongues of fire appearing in the air, sound effects from heaven, and the miracles of God declared in all the languages of the visitors to the city. The disciples have been expecting something like this, and someone must explain it to the puzzled crowd before they get the wrong end of the stick.

It is at this point that Peter climbs up before the crowd and 'speaks into the fear and chaos with a sacred word'. Faced with such unprecedented events, people crave an explanation from a man or woman to whom God has spoken. Peter had not been a great orator hitherto, and had a considerable talent for inserting his foot into his own mouth! However, on this occasion he speaks up bravely for his Lord, applying the Word of God to this strange situation with great effect. Far from being bored, the crowd are profoundly grateful, and several thousand of them press forward, demanding to know what they should do next.

Of course, the other great example in the Bible of preaching as articulation of God's deeds is Jesus himself. We only have the record of one sermon that he preached, but in it he shows how the preacher takes familiar words and an unfamiliar situation and brings them together. The people who gathered round him on a hill overlooking Lake Galilee had been brought up on the Old Testament scriptures. Day after day they had prayed, like their grandparents before them, that the Messiah would come. Now he was standing there before them. What should they do about it? If the Messianic age really had come, how should they behave? Time and time again in the Sermon on the Mount, Jesus takes words from their spiritual heritage and applies them to their everyday experience. 'It is written' would have been a very familiar phrase to them by the time they went home that day! Among these spiritually hungry but equally confused people, God chooses to use the means of preaching to address their needs.

What we can see is that there is ample evidence that God uses preaching as a means of motivation and explanation in the story of scripture. What we shall go on to see, however, is that it did not stop after the canon of scripture was closed. Preaching has played a role in the history of the Church, and arguably in the history of the world, as an agent of change.

Historical precedent

To review the entire history of preaching would take a whole series of books, and if you read them all you would have no time to preach anyway! The intention here is to look at a few key examples where preaching has played a key role as an agent of change.

As you read this book, great changes are afoot in Europe and elsewhere. The political map with which many of us grew up is changing. Old alliances have been broken and new ones formed. A political shift is under way. These changes, however, are a mere tremor compared to the earthquake which was rocking Europe in the fifteenth century. A spiritual revolution, started by Martin Luther, shook the foundations of both church and state. Everyone, from barons and princes to ploughmen and farm boys, found themselves uncertain about what was going on. Were they saved or weren't they? Did the Church hold the keys to heaven and the tickets out of purgatory, or was salvation available directly from God? When a peasant taking part in one of Luther's radical masses in Wittenberg dropped the chalice and was aghast to think that he might have spilled the *actual* blood of Christ on the ground, he reflected a far more widespread confusion.

At this point, enter the preachers. Although men like Luther, Calvin and Zwingli were essentially theologians, they were also preachers. Calvin, in particular, set great store by the importance of preaching. He saw the preacher as an interpreter, essential to the well-being of the believer: 'God is pleased to address us after the manner of men by means of interpreters, that he may thus allure us to himself, instead of driving us away by his thunder'. Luther urged his students to root their preaching in the everyday experience of their listeners so as to connect with them. These men recognised that, in a moment of stupendous change, the ordinary believer needed someone to take their hand and lead them through the quaking landscape. That someone was the preacher, and still is.

Several centuries later, another great change was on the way. As power shifted and views changed, the sun was setting on the slave trade. However, it would not go down without a fight, and there were preachers who saw fit to join in with that fight. Baptist preachers urged their congregations from the pulpit to vote only for abolitionist politicians in the general election. Their influence was enormous, and helped to bring about the withdrawal of Britain from the slave trade. At the time, the preachers had an education which was denied to many in their congregations. As learned men, it was incumbent on them to pass on to their people an understanding of world events and what the Bible had to say about them. These preachers recognised that they were agents of change in God's hands.

Another century, another struggle. With black Americans suffering terrible privations and injustice, there was an acute need for people to know what God had to say about it. At this point, Martin Luther King entered the fray. As a called and anointed preacher of God's word, he was able to bring an incisive Biblical perspective to bear upon the civil-rights struggle. Although his most famous speech was given outside a church context, the sermons that he preached in church ring with the power and zeal of a man on a mission. In such momentous times, there is a great need for the voice of God to be heard.

Our last preacher has not been associated with political change, but rather with the change of hundreds of thousands of individual lives. Although he has a reputation as the confidant of presidents and statesmen, it is the effect of his preaching on individuals which has done more to bring about radical change than anything else. I refer, of course, to Dr Billy Graham. In the course of his life, he has preached to more of the world's population than any other human being. The Billy Graham

Association estimates the figure at over 210 million people in over 185 countries and territories. He began his ministry in a day when few had telephones or televisions, and has continued into the age where people can carry both around with them! His straightforward preaching style, without visual aids or any other kind of adornment, has proved incalculably powerful. The overall effect of these changed lives, and of the lives they go on to change, has been enormous on the history of planet Earth.

All this is evidence that the God who had a place for preaching in the days of the scripture still has one for it now. The reason he called you, and others like you, is that the job still needs to be done.

We must ask now what it is that makes preaching so necessary. Why has God chosen to make use of it over the centuries? Why does it still have a place when so many other means of communication have altered beyond all recognition? The answer is partly to be found in our psychological make-up and partly in our spiritual make-up.

Psychological make-up

To return to Billy Graham for a moment, one might have thought that these days the Billy Graham Association would do better to send out an interactive CD-ROM with integral response section rather than going to all the trouble of organising crusades. Wouldn't sound-bites, video and music be a better way to reach us? The answer, drawn from experience, is a resounding 'no'. God has so designed us that we are drawn in and touched by live speech in a way that other mediums fail to do. Despite all our sophistication, there is still something within us that is captivated by another person speaking from the heart. Western politics in recent years has shown how much we like passionate conviction and how little we respect scripted spin.

Particularly when it comes to matters of life and death, we have an instinctive distrust of the mechanical and impersonal. There are certain things which we will not believe unless another human being tells them to us. If you have had cause to contact a hospital, for instance, and have found yourself working through an automated telephone menu, you will know exactly what I mean! Even when it is possible for people to speak to each other through mobile video calls, there are still some things which simply have to be said face to face.

Spiritual precedent

Of course, this reflects not only our psychological make-up but also our spiritual make-up and heritage. Ours is a faith based on the speech of God to his creation from beginning to end. When the world came into being as God's big idea, it was communicated through live speech – and things started happening. The hymn-writer Caroline Noel, in her hymn 'At the Name of Jesus', captured it beautifully with the words 'at his voice creation sprang at once to sight'. In other words, the sound of his voice made things happen, bringing life and beauty where there had been only emptiness. He went on to employ prophets of all shapes and sizes to pass on his message through their words and actions. Instead of using some kind of heavenly postal service, he insisted on using a courier every time. Every one of God's messages was delivered in person, from Moses' 'let my people go' to Christ's 'I am the way'. We should expect such a God to use personal messengers to this day.

Consider the parable of the vineyard for a moment. A man owns a vineyard of which he is inordinately proud. Over the years, it has been nurtured and tended so that it yields the finest of grapes. Although he is at a distance from it, he feels very deeply about it and cares about its future. The time has come to get a message through to those who work the vineyard for him. Do you remember the story? In his desperation to get the message through, the owner sends a whole string of servants to speak to the workforce. Each one is rebutted with violence until at last he sends his son, who is killed. It is a story of God's love expressed in Jesus, but also of the store he sets by personal and costly communication of his messages.

There can be little doubt from what we have seen that God does have a place for preaching. Our psychological and spiritual make-up demands it, and the history of the Church and the Bible has led us to expect it. However, the fact that there is a place for preaching does not mean that there is a place for *bad* preaching!

What's so bad about preaching?
Presumptions

Some years ago, a very young girl commented on how she would like to have my job because it meant that she could 'stand at the front of the church and talk a lot'. In fact, there are many preachers who enjoy their talking more than others enjoy listening! Sometimes this is because they presume too much upon their relationship with those to whom they preach. Firstly they feel, like the little girl, that their audience is a captive one with no choice but to listen to them. Secondly, they presume that their other work among the congregation, be it pastoral or organisational, has won them the right to be heard. Many fine pastors assume that the undoubted quality of their pastoral work will outweigh the inadequacies of their preaching work. Sadly, the person whose hand they held at the hospital bed will not necessarily have their attention held in the pulpit because of what has gone before. Preaching in a local congregation which is unsupported by care for that congregation is unworthy of the name. However, careless preaching which presumes upon the preacher's relationship with those who listen actually undermines that relationship. If I really love these people, shouldn't my care be expressed in the way I address them as well as the way I care for them?

I refer, of course, not just to the tone in which they are addressed but to the care given to preparing that address. A shoddy sermon is like a shoddy piece of furniture – unattractive and unlikely to support the weight of those who rely on it! There is a certain bravado among some preachers about their ability to 'wing it'. Just as anglers are inclined to boast about 'the one that got away', preachers may boast about 'the one I got away with'. Tales of burning the midnight oil on a Saturday night are exchanged with a knowing wink from one professional to another. The worthiness of such an approach, however, is highly questionable. If preaching really stands within the fine Biblical and historical tradition which we have described, how dare we treat it in such a cavalier fashion? Not only this, but to suggest that our congregations are too stupid to notice our lack of preparation is to undermine the very relationship that preaching is meant to express!

Sometimes it is not the reading of our Bibles which reveals a lack of preparation, but the reading of our congregations. In January 1998, the UK Prime Minister Tony Blair told a group of blank-faced Japanese businessmen that the British government would go 'the full Monty' in establishing the British economy. Not surprisingly, they had not seen the film of the same name, and hadn't the faintest clue what he was talking about! When you are faced with similarly blank faces, it may be because you have failed to read your audience in exactly the same way. Unfortunately, preachers are renowned for their ability to scratch where people don't itch and to answer the questions they weren't asking anyway. We need to make sure that we avoid both presuming on our listeners' good nature and making undue presumptions about their needs and concerns.

Detractors

Many preachers feel like a tin duck at a fairground, passing across the pulpit as the congregations train their rifles, and expecting to be knocked down on a regular basis. Not only this, but they also feel that bigger guns are trained on them from the distance. Some such guns are in the hands of the media, with their slick presentation and their big budgets. Others are in the studies of the theologians, as they analyse the relevance of preaching in the contemporary setting. Yet others are in the hands of famous people, making fun of the plodding preacher in his or her small cause. Like many of our fears, some of these owe more to paranoia than fact. However, if we simply hope they will go away, we shall be disappointed. Frightened preachers do little to earn their listeners' respect and much to earn the world's mockery. Let's look these critics in the eye, assess what they have to say, and decide how much notice to take of it.

The mass media

Two cows were standing in a field one day munching the sweet grass. They both looked up as a gleaming milk tanker drove past the field on its way from the dairy. On its side was emblazoned the message: 'fresh milk: pasteurised, homogenised, vitamins added'. One cow turned to the other and said: 'Makes you feel kind of inadequate, doesn't it?'

Before they come to church on a Sunday morning, many of your congregation will have watched news reports from around the world. These reports will have been beamed into their homes from distant places using satellite technology. Not only will the news be bang up to date, but also it will be presented in an interesting format, slickly introduced and lavishly illustrated with maps and graphics to make it accessible. Those of the congregation who were not watching the news may well have been playing computer games or surfing the Internet. There they will have seen high-quality graphics and interesting pictures galore. Once they get to church, they are confronted by you, your Bible and, if you are fortunate, a data or overhead projector. It's easy to feel, like the cow in the old story above, 'kind of inadequate'.

You probably feel envious of the television's ability to support every word which is said with graphics. Rather than relying on the power of verbal description, as you must, there are camera crews and vision mixers to make things interesting. Not only this, but also the television producers can change the images every few seconds in order to stay ahead in the constant battle with waning concentration. The pace is constantly varied, from sober analysis and dry statistics to shocking images and sweeping vistas. Not easy to reproduce from a pulpit! Furthermore, the television producers have an army of researchers and correspondents at their disposal, not to mention an array of special effects and graphics programmes of which you can only dream.

However, before you plunge off into such a sea of despair that you become a news story yourself, just pause and think. What makes the most captivating form of television, or for that matter of journalism? Story is the key. People are fascinated by people. The best kind of journalism is the kind that allows us to understand a global situation through a personal story. The most engaging vehicle for drama on stage or screen is the stories of people. This plays to our advantage, since the Bible is full of stories of people. In it, theological truth is turned into reality as people, both good and bad, experience God. You have a resource which would be the envy of many a scriptwriter. This is a resource which we shall plunder for all it is worth in the chapters which follow.

The theologians

There are some contemporary theological thinkers who are saying that the sermon no longer has a valid place in the life of the Christian Church. They have increased in number since people started describing this as the postmodern age. We are told that, in an age where an overarching story or 'metanarrative' has gone out of fashion, we cannot expect to preach from the Bible any more. Some would point to the failure of the churches either to stem their own loss of people or to reverse the moral decline in society. 'Preaching doesn't work', they say. Many post-evangelicals are post-preachers too.

Some challenge preaching on the grounds of competing metanarratives. They point to conflicts in the Middle East and the Balkans, where one person's view of reality has been imposed upon another's, with bloody consequences. In the light of this, they suggest that we should stick to the safer ground of general moral teaching that addresses the human condition. They would argue that religious preaching has often fanned the flames of conflict between groups, and that it therefore has no place in a multicultural society. Theirs is a call not to stir things up.

Others challenge preaching on psychological grounds, arguing that our human make-up is such that we learn better through doing than through listening. If this is so, they say, Christians who passively listen to sermons will not internalise the things they hear, and therefore will not be enabled to live Christian lives. Research by the Evangelical Alliance and the London Institute for Contemporary Christianity has identified the inability of many Christians to articulate their Christianity in the workplace, and blames this partly on ineffective preaching.

A similar argument is to challenge preaching on educational grounds. Changes in the educational environment have moved the classroom emphasis from a teacher's monologue to a teacher–student dialogue. Much more learning takes place now in interactive learning and discussion groups than it does simply in passive listening. If we understand preaching as teaching, then we should take due note of this clash in styles between the Church and other learning environments.

One other theological argument brought to bear on this issue is that of the Church as interdependent community. Our beliefs about every-member ministry mean that we are uncomfortable with placing too much emphasis on any one individual. Some argue that the seated congregation, all facing an individual at the front of their gathering and listening passively to what he or she is saying, undermine our beliefs that we are all equally gifted and equally important.

There are answers to all these arguments, some of which are set out below. It's not just 'fighting off' the arguments which matters, though. As a preacher, as a person who devotes time, energy and not a little anguish to the act of preaching, there is something you should remember. If the theologians hadn't asked these questions about psychology and ecclesiology and education – *you* should have done! An unthinking preacher is a liability. Don't be afraid to examine the questions, even if you come up with answers very different to theirs.

When dealing with these philosophical questions, don't be too overawed. The jury is still out on postmodernism, and the case is by no means proven. Postmodernism itself is not a populist movement, but has its origins in esoteric French philosophy. The philosophers involved with it argue that the world now operates differently, and that we no longer understand it through an overarching story. They explain this in many books and seminars by telling ... the same overarching story! Human beings do in fact make sense of the world by use of a metanarrative, be it Christian, Muslim or pagan. The human race has not changed so much with the progress of technology and the information revolution that we have lost the need for a basis on which to interpret our environment. If you began your Christian life believing that the Bible had proved its reliability on historical and experiential grounds, there is no need to abandon that belief now. Of course you will want to adapt your preaching of it to the world as it has become. Of course you will preach differently in a multi-ethnic, multicultural setting from the way that your forebears might have done. However, you should not feel that the Bible itself is to be hidden away like a guilty secret from an earlier age.

The question about competing metanarratives or world-views is a valid one. We live in an age where terrorists around the world have embraced martyrdom and cited God's word as their reason for doing so. Whether that word is the Koran or the Bible makes little difference to those outside the churches who look on with perplexity and fear. When a radical Muslim cleric is threatened with deportation for inciting religious hatred through preaching, preachers of every kind find themselves preaching cautiously. Secular authorities have started to recognise the capacity of preaching to shape and motivate those who listen to it. In happier circumstances, we would probably welcome this as a good thing – to see preachers treated with respect rather than derision. In these circumstances, though, preachers have often turned instead to preaching which can best be described as harmless. However, for Christian preachers, bland moralising is not the only alternative to polemical preaching. In our hands, we have God's radical manifesto for global change, with the Gospel of Christ at its heart. Sensitively preached, there is ample need for this world-view. It is our sacred duty to communicate it, although we would never seek to enforce it.

The degree to which we are influenced by the psychological and educational arguments depends on our view of preaching. If the preacher's role is primarily to exhort, then we can make sure that there are other opportunities to educate in the life of the Church. However, if we see preaching as education, then we must give a fair hearing to the arguments about its limitations. That said, when a significant amount of information needs to be communicated in a limited time, live speech from one person to many can still have great effect. Many degree courses, for example, still rely heavily on the lecture format. Although it is complemented by many other learning techniques, it is still an important part of the teaching. For passing on factual data and key principles, it has much to commend it, so long as it is well done. While small groups create great opportunities for interaction, they can often prove variable in the quality of learning and understanding which they provide.

The theological argument about the entire congregation should not really cause us many problems. After all, if we pursued it too far, we would have to have several people praying, several people reading the Bible, and, dare we say, several organists playing all at once! The concept of every-member ministry does not mean that everybody should do everything but rather that everybody should do something and that nobody should do nothing. The fact that one preaches and many listen need not undermine the communal nature of the Church. That said, the preacher should always avoid a tone which suggests that he or she is right and everybody else is wrong. Such a tone is certainly corrosive to the fellowship life of the Church.

The congregation

Of course, however careful you are about your tone and content, your preaching will still meet with a mixed response. Some will love it and not tell you so, while others will hate it and tell you so – and a vast group in the middle will seem so unmoved that it is hard to say what they think. The handshake and thank-you at the church door can be as meaningless as a politician's smile for the camera – insincere but necessary. When people do actually comment on our preaching, we should be grateful for the response. However, it is always hard to accept criticism willingly. Why did they criticise your preaching today? There are a number of possible reasons.

You deserved it. Perhaps your sermon was hastily put together with little or no research. Despite your belief in your own ability to fool them, they have seen through your lack of preparation. Alternatively, you may have made a clumsy application to what you think is the reality of their daily lives. In fact, you are wide of the mark, and they resent such a careless description of the lives they lead. Or perhaps you used a familiar preacher's short-cut – replacing compassion with combustion! With no time to research a clever way into their hearts, you have blasted your way through their defences with accusations and guilt bombs. You have even taken it upon yourself to raise a laugh or two by illustrating the shortcomings of the Christian with some thinly disguised descriptions of individual foibles within the congregation. Now that the sermon is over, put yourself in their shoes. How would *you* feel? These kinds of criticisms can be taken away to a quiet place and learnt from for another occasion.

You invited it. Maybe you adopted a tone of superiority rather than authority in the pulpit today. Whichever it was, the fact of the matter is that your own spiritual walk is so out of touch with God that you are in no position to dispense pearls of your own wisdom. We all go through times of spiritual dryness when the pulpit still beckons and Sunday comes around. We must make sure, however, that on those occasions we dispense only Biblical wisdom and not our own jaded insight. We may be in danger of becoming like the preacher described by Chrysostom as 'unable to confer any real benefit upon the congregation because he has nothing useful to say'.[2] In preaching, we proclaim God's authority – but we should not rely too much upon our own.

They weren't listening. It is equally possible that someone found your sermon dull or confusing or uninteresting simply because they weren't listening. Their mental state may have been such that they were unable to listen because of all the multiple concerns on their mind. Alternatively, they may have been in such a poor state of spiritual health that they would not have been inclined to listen to God even if he sat down in front of them. Of course, you must try to make them interested and to hold their attention. However, the Bible is very clear on each man's and woman's individual responsibility for their spiritual welfare. They may have put themselves out of touch with God – in which case you will have to help them through means other than the pulpit.

They were listening. The most violent negative reactions to preaching often occur when it is well honed and targeted rather than being vague and boring. I refer to those occasions when a preacher hits a raw nerve in his listener and gets a negative reaction as a result. If you have seen this even once as a preacher, you will remember it for the rest of your life. When it happens, you may well find that there is little verbal response to your sermon. Alternatively, people will pick up on very minor points of detail in order to disguise their more deep-rooted unease. On these occasions, their response should be an encouragement to you as a preacher – although it takes a lot of grace to handle it well.

In the end, it is the sense of call which prevails against all these odds. No-one welcomes critics, be they real or imagined. However, if the burden to preach is strong enough, it outweighs all of them. If you know in your heart that there is not only a place for preaching in the kingdom but also for you as a preacher, then read on. If you love to see hungry Christians fed, but you hate to give them stale bread, then read on.

Chapter 2

Txt u l8r

Before we rush to a solution for the preaching malaise, we have to recognise that language itself, without which we cannot preach, is changing. Since the late 1980s, letters have given way to faxes, and faxes have given way to e-mails. Meanwhile, SMS or text messaging, the young upstart on the communication scene, has stolen the show. Every month in the UK alone, 1 billion of these messages are exchanged. Some are vital, others inconsequential, and many welcome. A whole new language has evolved to enable communication with the greatest economy of letters. Although a text version of the Lord's Prayer does exist, and the Australian Bible Society has produced the whole Bible in text style, we have not yet seen the phenomenon of the text sermon.

However, some preaching is either so soulless that it might as well be in this mini-speak, or so bald in its use of language that it makes text look complex by comparison! What has happened to the truly great orators, the people who could make a crowd gasp with the majesty of their imagery or sob with the pathos of their poetry? What has happened to the day when preachers were the people setting the linguistic trend with their mastery of the English language? Perhaps it is not only speaking but also listening which has changed. Writing in the *Guardian* in September 2006, Guy Browning commented that 'many people's lives are devoid of concentration. Modern culture is served up in small, easily digestible chunks that require the attention span of a gnat' (© Guardian News and Media Ltd, 2006). In such a context, we often applaud the use of short sermons which pander to our downsized attention spans. However, a short sermon need not be an abbreviated sermon. The preacher should still take the time that he or she needs to say what they want to say, and to say it well!

Poetry and text are at opposite ends of the spectrum. The one has removed every trace of adornment in a bid for economy of characters. The other chooses every word carefully, for the sake not of economy but of impact. A poet may take hours choosing the right word, just like a cabinet-maker selecting wood with just the right grain for his masterpiece. The hours of labour by either craftsman are repaid by the impact of the finished article. A poetic preacher preaches 'the lamb of God who looks like something hung up at the butchers' (Fred Buechner, cited in Mitchell, p. 38).[3] If that image makes you shudder, it is because the writer intended it to. However, we can be fairly sure that he thought long and hard about exactly how to provoke our interest and revulsion in the choice of those few words.

Many congregations bemoan overly formal preaching where the preacher has his head stuck in his notes and fails to establish eye contact with the listeners. In a welcome bid for noteless informality, too many preachers have settled for a language which is bland, insipid and altogether uninspiring. This is hardly surprising, since few can be expected to produce truly lyrical language 'off the cuff'. They feel that a careful selection of language and images in advance would leave them open to the accusation of non-spontaneity, like a person in a prayer meeting disturbing the spontaneous silence by unfolding their 'script'.

We need to look around at those forms of communication which move people the most. While it may sometimes be an entirely spontaneous outburst, this is by no means the rule. Think of a film which has moved you deeply. A script has been carefully drafted and redrafted. Each scene has been shot with attention to the minutest detail. The actors and actresses have been selected from thousands of hopefuls because of their ability to make a story seem real. Movie-making does not just 'happen'. Nor do novels ... or paintings ... or sculptures. While our preaching should always have the immediacy of a conversation, there is no reason why it should not also have the artistry of a masterpiece. After all, our aim is to gain both hearts *and* minds, is it not?

The paucity of language in preaching

If we are agreed that preaching is intended to move as well as to inform, and that it should touch the heart as well as challenge the mind, how do we explain the descent into prosaic or even banal language which dogs so much preaching? Why is it that we expect more poetry and drama in a political address than in a sermon? There was a day when the greatest orators were to be found in the churches, and thousands hung on their words both 'live' on the Sunday and printed in the newspapers on a Monday. What went wrong? Of course, there are all sorts of reasons why the numbers listening to sermons have dropped, some of which are far outside the scope of this book. However, our interest here is particularly to discover why the linguistic style of preaching has veered away from the poetic and towards the prosaic.

Education

While I do not wish for one moment to join the 'make-them-learn-Shakespeare' brigade, it is probably true that many preachers today forget great literature the moment they leave formal education behind. In fact, for many, by the time they enter formal ministerial formation, even reading literature for pleasure is a thing of the past. The demands of the job and the need to keep up with the latest theological literature means that leisure reading is squeezed out. As a result, their personal vocabulary is less and less shaped by the finest 'architects' of the English language. It's not so much that they don't quote poetry and literature, which can seem very artificial anyway; it's more that such literature fails even to shape their language. Once this trend is set, and they then receive formal training in theology, church history and the like, it is hard for poetry to find a way back into their thoughts, and from there into their language. The net result of much theological training is a style of preaching which is heavily propositional – whereby 'propositions' or truths are handed down to the congregation from the pulpit. This tends to be expressed in the kind of prosaic language which leaves little room for poetry.

Overwork

Very few preachers have the luxury of preaching as their sole ministry. By the time they stand up to deliver their sermon on a Sunday, they have chaired meetings, visited the sick, resolved disputes, balanced budgets and made plans. In such a busy life, even finding time for sermon-preparation can be hard. When that preparation is fitted in around other things, and when it is being done at the end of a long week and a short fuse, creativity is the first victim. As time goes on and sermon-preparation suffers, some make themselves intentionally busier and busier with other worthwhile things. That way, if the sermon is not well received, at least there is the perfect excuse for its lack of success. Who will argue with a preacher whose sermon gave way to a vital pastoral visit? The intense pressure of the preaching and pastoral environment can sometimes lead to this kind of rationale.

Let us suppose that I am preparing a sermon for Sunday morning. It is Friday lunchtime, and I already have an all-day booking for tomorrow. I have read my Bible passage and collected my thoughts on it. I know pretty much what I should say to the congregation. Now I have a choice. I can either express these truths in the prosaic language which comes readily to hand, or I can roll up my sleeves and go exploring at the back of the linguistic cupboard. It's dark in there, and it takes time to find every word. Often, I will have to fish each one out, dust it off and hold it up to the light before deciding whether it will do the job. Before I know where I am, two hours have elapsed and the sermon is only half-written. No wonder we often reach for the words at the front of the shelf!

Biblical illiteracy

At the back of my desk drawer, I have a medal awarded for scripture knowledge to some anonymous scholar in years gone by. The yellow and purple of its ribbons have faded with age, and the brass on its bar has gone dull with the passage of years. Everything about it speaks of a bygone age – an age when families went to church together, an age when Bible classes were full, and an age when Bible knowledge was something to be proud of. Today, many preachers face a congregation on a Sunday where many of those listening know little about their Bibles. Some of the reasons for this are cultural – the younger ones in the congregation have been brought up in an era where the Bible has little place in national life. Some of it is to do with lifestyle – the busy people in front of them have little time to read anything, whether the Bible or anything else. Some of it is to do with spiritual discipline – they simply do not regard Bible-reading as a priority. Whatever the reasons might be, the net result is that many preachers face congregations who are highly educated but Biblically ignorant, or whose computer literacy is far in excess of their Biblical literacy. This means that they are unable to make connections between Biblical principles and passages, and that their awareness of how scripture fits together is very limited. In such a context, the preacher often feels that he or she has a lot of remedial educational work to do. The sermon must accommodate not only exhortation and persuasion but a good deal of education too. Bluntly put, if people will not make sense of the Bible for themselves, the preacher must do it for them. In such a situation, unambiguous and prosaic language is bound to come to the fore.

Every-member ministry

You may be surprised to see this listed as a problem. It is, surely, something which we hold dear – the idea that every man and woman in the kingdom has their own contribution to make to its growth? Within the local church, this is expressed on a Sunday, for example, as some lead prayers, some arrange flowers, some play music, some welcome visitors and some preach. However, in a context of vibrant every-member ministry, some preachers actually feel very threatened. The lessening emphasis on the exaltation of the preacher as one with a *singularly* important ministry makes them feel quite insecure. When it does, they often feel that they must defend the bastion of the preacher's uniqueness by loading the cannon of the sermon with the heftiest intellectual shot they can find! When the sermon is laden with cerebral material and delivered in prosaic and authoritarian language, it is often the preacher's attempt to ensure that their unique contribution is respected.

Political correctness

I write this today in a world which has seen the ugly face of religious extremism. Far from treating it as harmless and risible, both politicians and journalists have realised the power of preaching to change hearts and minds. When powerful preachers of whatever faith are arrested for 'radicalising' their audiences and leading them to do dangerous and destructive things in the name of faith, preaching is recognised as a powerful weapon. This is a fact now enshrined in law within the UK, where preaching religious hatred is a crime. In such a context, many preachers are acutely aware of their vocabulary. For the best of motives, they have 'toned down' their preaching – but the result is insipid and bland to the point of being utterly harmless. This has happened with the rise of politically correct language too. While Christians should be the first to applaud linguistic reform which forbids derogatory descriptions of anyone on the grounds of race, creed or sexuality, the result has often been a paralysing fear among those who open their mouths in public. Rightly concerned about saying the wrong thing, they end up saying very little indeed. What they do say is couched in the most ordinary of language, where words are chosen for their obvious meaning. The kind of creative ambiguity, or polyvalence, which poetry lives and breathes cannot thrive in such a restricted environment.

Scriptural correctness

In an age of political correctness where fear of religious extremism runs rife, the pressure on the preacher to be Biblically accurate is great. With a high regard for the authenticity of the Word of God, our desire is to let it speak as accurately and fully as possible. However, in seeking not to deviate from the text, we end up with sermons which keep its letter but destroy its spirit. When this happens, all the preacher's desires to tackle Biblical illiteracy and to give a positive message in an arid spiritual environment can come to nothing. It is perfectly possible, for instance, to preach a sermon on Christ's sovereignty as displayed in the calming of the storm which is extremely accurate, but which captures neither the terror of the storm nor the wonder of his power. We desperately need the kind of language which makes people feel as well as making them think.

Reversing the trend

Education

If it is important for literature to feed the mind as well as for scripture to feed the soul, then preachers must be encouraged to do both. On a personal level, you can change this by adapting your personal timetable and habits to accommodate some time for reading for pleasure. If you really believe that this will benefit your preaching, then there is no need to regard it as 'wasted' time. Although it may seem indulgent when you first begin, you will soon find that it is an investment in the preaching task. Perhaps it is time for the training colleges to show a lead here too. What could they do to encourage students of the Word to be students of lesser words too? Can courses and syllabi in the colleges encourage students to learn from the linguistic dexterity and poetic richness of non-theological writers?

Overwork

It may be that overwork is endemic to the local minister's life. As we have seen, sometimes we actually make ourselves busier in order to defend against the charge of ill-prepared preaching. However, history has taught that Spirit-driven, dynamic preaching can affect far more than the Sunday life of the Church. Truly great preaching can affect lifestyles and moral choices, releasing financial and personal resources and energising the Church of Christ. It can act as a kind of preventative pastoral care too – offering the kind of guidance which will head off the pastoral crisis before it happens. Habits are always hard to change, but when change happens in the right direction it certainly pays dividends. Although it will be hard at first to invest the extra time in your preaching required to select poetic and evocative vocabulary instead of the ordinary words which come straight to hand, won't it be worth it if the congregation sits up and takes notice? Time spent crafting a sermon which changes the lives of all those who hear it will yield far more results than any number of committee meetings or planning sessions.

Biblical illiteracy

There is no denying that this is a real problem. Attitudes and lifestyles have combined to produce a Biblical illiteracy of which our forefathers would have been ashamed. However, dry didactic sermons are not the only way to tackle it. If we can learn to release the dynamic power both of the little stories and of the overall story of the Bible, then we will create a Biblical hunger which God's Spirit will help us to fill. If we can send people home thrilled by the story of Jesus calming the storm or touched by the story of Ruth's loyalty, this may do far more to encourage their Bible-reading than any thematic sermon on sovereignty or loyalty might have done.

Every-member ministry

When we flatten the landscape of the Church by saying that because everybody matters a little nobody matters much, we are doing a great disservice to the Kingdom. Although the exaggerated exaltation of the preacher as the person with all the answers is unhelpful, the suggestion that the role of preacher does not really matter is equally unhelpful. The preacher *does* have a special calling. He or she is called upon to act as a mouthpiece, communicating the very heartbeat of God to those who have come hungrily into his house. This is the reason for James's stern warning that 'not many of you should presume to be teachers, my brothers, because you know that we who teach will be judged more strictly' (James 3:1). If you are called to this role, then you should be so sure of it in your heart that you do not need to bolster it in any other way.

Political correctness

Preachers should be as sensitive as anybody else to the need for appropriate language. In comparison to politicians and broadcasters, they should be even more careful about choosing language which does not cause unnecessary offence. However, there is such a thing as *necessary* offence, and the preacher should not be afraid of causing it. Martin Luther was profoundly offensive when he criticised the Church of his day, nailing his ninety-five theses to the door of the church in Wittenberg. Centuries later, Martin Luther King was equally offensive to the racist establishment when he laid an axe to the root of their tree. While preaching should not go out looking for contention, it should not be afraid of it either. In the end, insipid preaching will create an insipid church, and such a church will not be able to help the world.

Scriptural correctness

The degree to which a preacher is troubled by this depends largely on the theological stable out of which they have come. Those from a conservative evangelical background will be keen to accord scripture the highest possible degree of respect. Not only this, but also they will be very wary of saying anything which might seem to undermine a literal interpretation of the Bible. While the motives of this are laudable, the end results are often disappointing. An accurate but dry exegesis of a psalm, for instance, ends up being inaccurate because it suggests to the listener that the psalm itself is dry and uninteresting. We must seek to be accurate in tone and feel as well as analysis if we are to do the Bible justice.

A time to speak

The writer of Ecclesiastes so many centuries ago said that there was a time for everything – whether speaking, keeping silence, making war or making peace. I believe that the time for lyrical preaching which stimulates the senses and engages the emotions has come of age. This may be the iPod generation, with their ear buds plugged in and their thumbs hovering over their keypad as they send texts by the thousand. However, it is also the Make Poverty History generation – where thousands were caught up in the seemingly dreary issue of world debt and international finance. How did it happen? By the use of high-profile media stars undoubtedly, but also through the clever communication of the individual stories on the sharp end of the debt crisis. It is also the Phoenix-the-calf generation. In 2001, large parts of Britain were in the grip of a foot-and-mouth crisis. Vast funeral pyres of dead cattle blackened the skies over much of Britain's farmland. When a small calf was found alive next to its dead mother, the story gripped the hearts of thousands. The fate of Phoenix the calf made a nationwide story personal, and it began a shift in policy on handling the crisis. Preach me a sermon today, and I am likely to feel offended or bored. Tell me a story, and I will at least give you the benefit of the doubt as I listen to it. We need to find a way of combining the two …

Chapter 3

A time for telling tales

In case you feel tempted at this point to close the book and dismiss it as a simple call to tell more stories in the pulpit and dumb down our sermons, let me reassure you. Of course, we have all heard stories used badly in the pulpit. We have heard endless preachers use a funny story to introduce their sermon, which then bears no relation whatsoever to the preaching which follows it. We have also suffered under the family-anecdote preacher – illustrating every point from his own family, to the detriment of congregation and family alike! We have also listened to sermons which were little more than a collage of stories loosely pasted together to paper over the theological cracks. We have endured, too, that particularly twenty-first-century phenomenon – the web-based story preacher. This style of preaching is heavily reliant on stories and anecdotes available under different themes online. The trouble is, everyone seems to fish in the same pond for their stories, and they come out over and over and over again. This is definitely not what I am advocating. Rather, I am looking for a more profound overhaul of the way we tackle preaching.

Narrative theology arises from a particular understanding of scripture on the one hand, and communication studies on the other. It sees stories as a potent vehicle for truth, rather than simply an illustration of that truth. It encourages the preacher to rely on the Biblical model of stories which are infused with truth, and to preach them for all they are worth. Used well, it can be a kind of stealth weapon in the preacher's armoury – creeping past the defences of the listener through the familiar medium of story, before unleashing the dynamic power of God's word.

Biblical roots

The Bible abounds with stories from start to finish – particularly the historical story of God's chosen people. Often we see that story repeated for the sake of preserving communal faith through the ages. The great Jewish festivals of Passover, Pentecost and Purim are all opportunities to rehearse again the story of God's relationship with his people. They also ensure that the story is passed on down the generations, as families gather round the table or in the synagogue. This is the big story of the Old Testament.

The prophets

In the prophets, however, we see smaller stories in use as a means of conveying God's truth. Sometimes this is through an enacted story, such as Ezekiel's construction of the model city of Jerusalem (Ezekiel 4–5) or Jeremiah's smashing of the jar in the city gate (Jeremiah 19). For Hosea, God's story was painfully bound up with his own as he and his wife went through a public separation, humiliation and reconciliation (Hosea 1–3). One of the most powerful sermons in the Old Testament is the one preached by Nathan the prophet to King David just after he had committed adultery with Bathsheba. Carefully, Nathan spins the story of a vulnerable farmer and his little baby lamb. David is so drawn into the story that, when the lamb is stolen, he leaps from his throne, incandescent with rage and calling for the culprit to be punished. It is at that point that Nathan says, I imagine in a dangerously quiet voice, 'you are the man' (2 Samuel 12:7). The Old Testament prophets were keenly aware that stories were a way to convey God's word not just to the minds but also to the hearts of their hearers.

Jesus

No-one can ever have had a more pressing agenda than Jesus to convey the heavenly truths of God. With only limited time, he had to undo centuries of theological misapprehension and lay the foundation for centuries of work in the Kingdom. How did he do it? Largely by telling stories. His Kingdom stories, or parables, worked on more than one level. To the unbelieving, they were intriguing stories, absorbing enough to make them listen and disturbing enough to make them think. To the faithful, meanwhile, they were full-colour descriptions of the Kingdom of heaven for them to cling onto. No-one can read the parables of Jesus and conclude that stories are not up to the job when it comes to conveying God's truth.

Epistles

For the most part, the Epistles consist of argument and persuasion rather than stories. However, there are one or two moments when the writers make use of stories within the community of the early Church to inspire and motivate. We see this in 2 Corinthians 8, for example, where Paul uses the story of the Macedonian Christians to goad the Corinthians into action. At this point, he believes that personal story rather than theological argument will win the day. In his third letter, John makes it clear that he has been repeating the story of Gaius' generosity, and encouraging others to do so, in order that the Church might learn from his example (3 John 3:5-6). These inspired leaders recognised the power of story as a motivator within the persecuted and scattered Church.

Revelation

It is to that same persecuted Church that the book of Revelation was delivered. It is likely that this seditious document was smuggled off the island of Patmos past the noses of John's captors. In it, he weaves a vivid story of God's final triumph and the devil's irreversible downfall. The story is not explained, but rather the images are left to speak for themselves. With a drama and vividness which most preachers would eschew, John shows what the end will be like. He certainly appreciated the power of story to touch both mind and heart.

Homiletical roots

The story of how narrative preaching has come about is a complex one. It is the product of wisdom, experience and theological reflection by minds much finer than mine. In what follows, I shall simply outline some of the steps which have led to its birth. For each step, several scholars and many books could be quoted, but instead I shall just mention one or two by way of example. You can then follow these up should you wish to know more.

Narrative theology

In the early 1980s, Robert Alter (*The Art of Biblical Narrative*) was one of many scholars to question how the Bible was read. Since the rise of historical criticism in the nineteenth and early twentieth centuries, Biblical scholars had been engaged on a quest to reconstruct the history behind the Biblical text in order to understand it fully. This was known as historical-critical theology, and combined the disciplines of textual criticism and historical research. However, Alter and others were asking: would it ever be possible to reconstruct that world out of which the text was born? Since we weren't there at the time, our knowledge is at best limited. Instead, Alter and others suggested that we should employ our efforts in understanding the text itself and how it functions, rather than asking unanswerable questions about where it came from. For the preacher, this means understanding how the text functions and what it does, and then seeking to imitate that in the sermon.

Form-sensitive preaching

Meanwhile, another debate had been going on within homiletical circles. In 1971, Fred Craddock started something of a homiletical revolution with his book *As One Without Authority*. Since the preacher had always been seen very much as a figure of authority, even the title was enough to cause controversy! Craddock's basic contention was that the preacher should respect not just the content of scripture but also its form. Our belief in inspiration means that we regard not just what scripture says, but also *how* it says it, as divinely inspired. The preacher does not have the authority to stand over the text and impose his or her sermonic style upon it. Rather, our quest as preachers should be to find a way of preaching a given text that echoes the style of that text. Thus, for example, a story should be preached as a story, and a piece of Pauline argument should be preached as a closely argued address. In this way, form-sensitive preaching was born.

Dramatic preaching

While Craddock was talking about the shape of scripture, Eugene Lowry had been thinking about the shape of the sermon. In his book *The Homiletical Plot*, published in 1978, he asked why so many sermons were so dull and predictable when they were based on the rich narrative material of the Bible. He pointed out that many propositional sermons were so predictable that those sitting in the pews simply did not bother to follow them to their inevitable conclusion. Narrative preaching should echo the intrigue, suspense and fascination of the original text in the form of the sermon. In short, it should keep people on the edge of their seats as much as a good novel or film does.

Linguistically rich preaching

Drawing on the insights of the Biblical scholars, and heeding the homiletical debate, men like Thomas Troeger and Walter Brueggemann have championed the cause of preaching that is not only sensitive to form and dramatic in shape but linguistically rich too. In his book *Imagining a Sermon*, Troeger traces the use of imagination within the Christian Church through the centuries, and calls on preachers to be every bit as creative in their language as the scriptwriters and copywriters outside the Church. Walter Brueggemann, an Old Testament scholar, calls for a return of stories to the pulpit: 'The deep places of our lives, places of resistance and embrace, are not ultimately reached by instruction. Those places are reached only by stories, by images, metaphors and phrases that line out the world differently.'[4] This is a skill which he demonstrates to great effect in his many volumes of published sermons.

Sermon as event

Looking at all of this, drawing on postmodern philosophy of language, and also analysing the power of preaching in the Black majority churches, has led many to call for a return to preaching as event. Jolyon Mitchell uses many of these insights, together with his years of experience in radio broadcasting, in his provocative book *Visually Speaking*. The sermon should be not just a body of words which is spoken, but also an event in which the Word is made manifest and the world is made different because of it. Seen like this, the sermon should be experienced as well as heard. It should be judged by its effect as well as its content. Also, it should touch the emotions and the imagination as much as it challenges the mind.

Narrative preaching

As outlined above, and shown in Figure 3.1 overleaf, narrative preaching is woven of many different strands. It arises from a debate about how we read scripture on the one hand, and how we communicate it on the other. It seeks to be true to the nature of scripture itself, but also to recognise the linguistic peculiarities of the world in which we live. For all our technological sophistication,

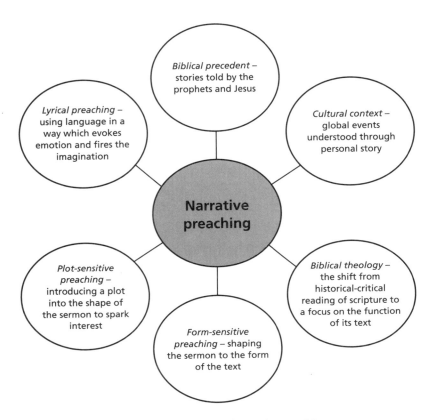

Figure 3.1: The origins of narrative preaching

we learn through stories just as much as our grandparents did, or even their grandparents before them.

Narrative preaching is the quest to unlock the power of the Bible's stories for a contemporary setting. This can be done in a number of different ways, using various approaches and different 'voices'. In Chapters 4–6, I shall outline three different ways in which it can be done. Each technique is explained first, and then illustrated through five annotated sermons. The sermons are reproduced as far as possible as they were preached – warts and all! Their strengths and weaknesses are analysed, and alternatives suggested on how else they might be preached. In these chapters, the theory of narrative preaching is put into practice 'on the ground', in order to assess how it works.

Chapter 4

Preaching with the first voice

July 2005 saw the city of London pitched into chaos by the savage bombings on the London Underground. As rescue and salvage teams laboured in the Stygian gloom below ground, so the death toll mounted. Picture editors were swamped by images supplied on every medium from mobile phones to high-end cameras. However, amid all the images and the worthy editorials, two voices rose up above all others. Though both were from very different backgrounds, both were united by one feature – their personal involvement in the tragedy.

George Psaradakis was the driver of the number 30 bus which exploded in Tavistock Square. One week after the outrage, he spoke at a memorial service to commemorate all those killed:

> A week ago, I took my No. 30 bus out from here on a journey which ended as a nightmare ... With quiet dignity and respect we show our deep contempt for those who planted the bombs and those who masterminded them.

While no different in character to the sentiments expressed by political and religious leaders elsewhere, Mr Psaradakis's words carried so much more power. This was because of his personal involvement in the event. These were words not of comment or sympathy; these were the testimony of an eye-witness. He was giving voice to his own experience and his reflections upon it.

Stale Bread?

Shortly afterwards, it was the turn of Marie Fatayi-Williams to take the stage. Having travelled all the way from Nigeria to look for her son who was lost in the bombing, she gave an impromptu press conference. With just a sheet of paper as a prompt, Mrs Fatayi-Williams gave vent to all the raw emotion of loss and grief that she felt as she cried out to know what had happened:

> I need to know, I want to protect him. I'm his mother, I will fight and die to protect him. To protect his values and to protect his memory. Innocent blood will always cry to God almighty for reparation. How much blood must be spilled? How many tears shall we cry? How many mothers' hearts must be maimed?

Others commenting on the bombings, whether government ministers from the dispatch box or preachers in their pulpits, would have been hard pushed to emulate the sheer emotional power of what she said. Who can equal or gainsay a mother's grief for her son? Marie's speech, which will be remembered for years to come, gains all its power from its personal connection with the events at hand. These are the words, not of a commentator or a pundit, but a person whose life is intimately bound up with the events concerned.

We saw this also in the wake of South-East Asia's dreadful tsunami in December 2004, as news teams across the world clamoured for every spare seat on a plane to take them to the disaster area. People most in demand were, of course, eye-witnesses. Even two or three weeks later, local newspapers in the UK and elsewhere gave front-page space to those who could testify to a personal experience of what had happened. Nothing beats the power of a first-person eye-witness account. Commenting on her many years as a foreign correspondent, Kate Adie writes that 'the technology changes, but the desire to record what it's like to witness history in the making does not, regardless of the hazards and hiccups in a correspondent's life'.[5]

It is maybe because of the power and immediacy of the first person as a narrative style that it is rarely used in literature. It comes across in such a raw form that the reader or listener can be overwhelmed by its power. It leaves little room for manoeuvre between the speaker and the listener. There has not been the same degree of processing which we might expect in a second-voice narrative. Time has not been taken to sift and analyse the events before giving them voice. Instead, the listener is left to feel that there is very little space between them and the events described – and even less between them and the speaker. This can be both an advantage and a disadvantage.

Benefits of using the first voice

When we consider using the first voice as a form in preaching, there are a number of advantages to consider. In the first instance, it injects exactly the kind of dynamism and energy seen in the examples above. It can enable the pulpit to crackle with danger and provocation instead of resounding with its more usual dull notes. By shortening the distance between the listener and the characters in the Old or New Testaments, it allows these characters to speak to the contemporary listener in a way which they have hitherto not done.

In an age of Biblical illiteracy, any form of preaching which turns the Bible's characters from two- into three-dimensional personae is a great advantage. It opens the ears of the listeners to voices which they have not previously heard and their eyes to new dimensions of the story. Not only this, but the preacher must also encounter the Biblical characters with an unaccustomed degree of thoroughness if he or she is going to attempt to 'get inside their head' in this way.

Often, as we have seen, preaching stands accused of not only being predictable and heavily propositional but also adopting a tone which is unacceptably dictatorial. In other words, it not only tells people what the Bible says – it also tells them what they ought to think about it! When a first-voice narrative is employed, this is much less likely to be a danger. A personal testimony is concerned with the opinions and experience of the person speaking, rather than an attempt to persuade the listener of a particular truth or point of view. Preachers who like to leave their listeners with a sparky ambiguity will find that the first voice serves them well.

Drawbacks of using the first voice

The first of these is exactly the same point made above. In a second-voice narrative, the text can be constructed in such a manner, with special points emphasised, that the listener can be directed in a particular way. This is even more the case with a third-voice sermon, where narrative is accompanied by more traditional preaching tools. In a true first-voice narrative, however, neither of these things can be done. The narrator must say his or her piece, and the consequences are left to the listeners – and to God, of course!

There is also a greater risk of unintentionally misleading the listeners. To speak on behalf of another person is always difficult. However, to do it on behalf of a dead Biblical character who cannot be consulted, and whose story we regard as part of the inspired Word of God, is even more risky! The corollary of this is that the first-person narrative probably demands more of the preacher in terms of homework than any other form. If we are to take the risk of speaking 'with another person's voice', it is incumbent upon us to find out as much as possible about them first.

Technique for using the first voice

Read the Word

Read the Word all you can. Read not only the principal story of the character you wish to portray, but every passing reference to them too. Get a Bible dictionary or a concordance, and look up every single Bible reference to your character. Make sure you don't miss any out, no matter how small. The best way to 'climb inside the head' of another person is to spend as much time as possible in their company. If this means reading a particular portion of the Bible again and again until it seems totally familiar, this can only be to the preacher's good.

Read the words

Today, the preacher has at their disposal all manner of reference sources. These might be Bible dictionaries, commentaries, background material on geography and culture, or the wealth of material available online. A careful perusal of these sources helps to 'flesh out' the story, and also helps to avoid anachronistic references in the text. A character should not, for instance, refer to the Temple when it was not built, or to Romans when they had not yet arrived! Think particularly about clothing, food, buildings and customs. These are the tiny details which will lend realism to your account. Try to read some of Tony Grant (ed.), *From Our Own Correspondent*, and to supply the kinds of details for your characters that those writers use.

Holy imagination

When we tackle this kind of narrative, it is impossible to do so without giving rein to our imagination. By its very nature, we are giving a voice to the Biblical story which is not present in the text. In order to find that voice, we shall have to drop our pitcher deep down into the wells of imagination. Many preachers are uncomfortable with this, for they feel it to be forbidden territory. Their discomfort, however, is surely unfounded. As Thomas Troeger points out in *Imagining a Sermon*, imagination has played a role in preaching since the very beginning. Furthermore, unless we believe that every word of our sermons is given to us verbatim by God, surely we are using our imagination whenever we preach, whether in this or a more traditional style? In using our imagination, we need to tap into all five senses if we can, thereby maximising our number of contact points with the listener.

Supplementary character

A technique worth employing from time to time in first-voice narratives is the use of a supplementary character. In this way, the sermon can tell a Biblical story with all the power and immediacy of an eye-witness account without the need for the key players to speak. There is an example of this in Sermon 4.1 below, 'Heaven scent', where the key characters are the wise men, but their story is told in the first person by an anonymous eye-witness. As is the case with all these techniques, it should not be used too often lest the listeners grow tired of the device.

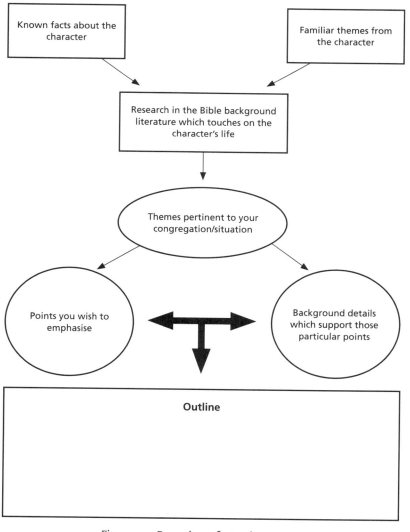

Figure 4.1: Preparing a first-voice sermon

Construction

It is important to remember that our aim is not simply to 'hear from' Joshua or Mary or whichever Biblical character we have selected. Rather, our aim, as with any other form of preaching, is to bring the Word to bear incisively on the lives of our listeners. If we simply tell the character's story, albeit in a colourful voice, we have failed to do so. In a state of prayer and under the guidance of God's spirit, we need to find a message for our listeners. Having found it, we then need to construct the sermon in such a way that we get the point across. As explained in Figure 4.1 overleaf, this theme-selection needs to take place early on in the process.

Sermon 4.1
Heaven scent (Matthew 2:1–12)

Context

This sermon was preached at a midnight service on Christmas Eve. In the congregation were both regular worshippers and those who only ever visit the church on this night of the year. The lateness of the hour means that both service and sermon are necessarily shorter than usual. The limited number of themes available for this particular service means that a different approach can be much appreciated. Unusually, on this occasion, a 'prop' was used – the stopper of an old perfume bottle.

Preparation

Read the Word

There is a limited amount that one can read about the actual story, given that it is covered only in a few verses of Matthew's gospel (2:1–12). Of particular significance was the instinctive reaction of awe and worship which the wise men showed on arrival at the stable. Herod's paranoia can be seen in this story, and also in the latter part of Matthew 2, where he institutes the murder of all the children under two years old in the Bethlehem area. Other valuable sources to read are the reactions of other individuals to the infant Jesus: the shepherds, Simeon and Anna.

Read the words

Biblical reference material can fill in a number of the gaps concerning the background of the wise men. It is possible to find out more about their background, their origins and even the kind of clothes they might have worn. Research on perfumes of the era can be useful too – giving you an idea of how they would have smelt. Any details about how the stable might have looked also helps to fix the setting in your imagination as a preacher.

Holy imagination

With the facts at your fingertips and the message in your heart, it is time to bring the two together with all the creativity you can muster. As you do so, remember that smell is among the most evocative of our five senses and can evoke a strong reaction in your listeners.

Supplementary character

Clearly, a supplementary character has been employed here. In order to bring out the themes of wonder, intrigue and even judgement, a character has been invented as an eye-witness. As you will see, he has a gruff nature and a past of which he is not entirely proud . . .

(Note: in each sermon that follows, the words in bold type are examined in the subsequent 'Analysis' section.)

Heaven scent (Matthew 2:1–12)

Now, you'll tell me it was wrong to keep this. And you'd be right. All these years, it's been in my possession, **wrapped up and carried close to my heart**. It was neither given to me nor intended for me, but now I have it. Every time I **hold** it in my hand, **feel** its delicate work, every time I **smell** its sickly perfume, still strong after all these years, my mind goes back to that strangest of nights.

Funnily enough, I smelt them before I saw them. There are many smells in the streets at the back of the palace, and few of them pleasant. But, when I caught a whiff of spice and myrrh on that night, I turned. What a sight. They may have left the palace by the back gate, but they were all dignity and poise. Their eyes darted everywhere, taking in this strange city and its little houses, some of them with a light flickering in the window. One of them spoke, clasping his treasure close to his chest in the folds of his robe. His voice was deep. 'He would have kept us from our quest, this puppet king', he said. 'A big man, to be so afraid of a little child', said the other. The third kept his

Analysis of Sermon 4.1

Now, you'll tell me it was wrong to keep this – a blunt, gruff introduction from a blunt, gruff character.

wrapped up and carried close to my heart – works on several levels, both physical and metaphorical.

hold . . . feel . . . smell – the importance of 'cashing in' on as many of the senses as possible. Background research reveals that it would have been a sickly, sweet smell. Bible encyclopaedias, Bible dictionaries, analyses of Old and New Testament times and their electronic equivalents can all all be useful here.

counsel, looking anxiously at the night sky. I followed them then, sometimes running, other times walking, never knowing if they knew I was there. When they reached an inn at the end of a back alley, there was nowhere left to hide. Instead I stood, like **a little boy gawping at his childhood sweetheart from afar**. And watched what happened next.

Stooping low, they all went into the stable at the back of the inn. There was a young woman in there, **just a teenager really**, nursing a baby with the most peaceful look on her face. You'd have thought she was running away from her father to have her child in such a place as this. But all seemed at peace. Then a look came over their faces, those three. It was a look like I had never seen. As they set eyes on the child, their faces changed. All the confidence, all the poise, all the dignity … it drained from them like the colour in the face of a man who is dying. And they knelt, knelt there in the straw. **Robes trailing in the muck. Soles of their feet bent back** like the pauper at prayer. Hands outstretched like a **beggar asking for alms**. This was an act of worship, nothing less.

Oh, how I wanted to join in. **How I wanted to rush in and blurt out that I was here and I knew I shouldn't be and not to be angry, but couldn't I just share my moment too?** But it passed. They gave their gifts to the young woman. Walked out past me, that whiff of spice brushing my shabby clothes as they went. **And were gone into the night**.

That's when I saw it, saw this. Glistening in the straw – the stopper from a perfume bottle. It was just by the door, just an arm's length away. And I wanted something of that heavenly moment for myself. She saw me take it, you know. Saw me reach in like a common thief and help myself to her priceless gift. And the strangest thing is, I'm sure the child saw me too. His tiny eyes

a little boy gawping at his childhood sweetheart from afar – works as an evocative description, but also to bridge the gap between this anonymous individual's world and the world inhabited by the listener. In first-voice narrative, there must be a great economy of language – many truths expressed through the one voice.

just a teenager really – likely to surprise many listeners, but likely to be true as well. This is the kind of thing that good research will reveal. Furthermore, it emphasises the gap between this vulnerable young woman in her simple surroundings, and the exotic and aged wisdom of the three.

Robes trailing in the muck – a reminder of the gritty reality of the stable setting – all too often sanitised out in Christmas celebrations.

Soles of their feet bent back – an uncomfortable image, both physically and emotionally. Bending the feet back in this way is uncomfortable and unnatural, especially the older we get. However, it is also an echo of the tradition in many religions, especially Eastern ones, of removing shoes in the presence of the holy.

beggar asking for alms – at points like this, our unknown narrator reveals the kind of depth that any preacher needs to have. These people were rich, and yet they were poor before the child. They came with gifts and wisdom, and yet they longed for blessing. The infant had more wisdom and power than all three of them put together. With careful work, the preacher can introduce a level of irony of which the character is unaware.

How I wanted to rush in and blurt out that I was here and I knew I shouldn't be and not to be angry, but couldn't I just share my moment too? – the rhythm of these staccato phrases is somewhere between the petulant child wanting their own way, and the traumatised victim punctuating their longing with sobs.

And were gone into the night – a phrase rich with Biblical echoes. It is used by Christ of his impending doom, and used by John when the door bangs shut behind Judas as he leaves to betray the holy one.

looked at me. And I felt that he saw me through and through. Saw every dark half-remembered deed. Saw every hope **twisted into disappointment**. Saw everything that might have been. In that split second, **my knees began to yield**. And I would have been on the floor like them. But the moment went, and I am here. **And this is mine**.

Positive aspects

Since many in the congregation were unaccustomed to church, they were surprised by such a different approach. It certainly appeared to hold their attention in a way that a more conventional sermon would not have done. Since the sermon was learnt by heart and 'performed' as a monologue, it had a certain element of theatre in it which was appreciated. The number of Gospel booklets taken by guests at the close of the service would suggest that many were touched by the dilemma that the character faced.

Negative aspects

Precisely because many of the listeners were unaccustomed to church, they struggled with the sermon. Without any appreciable Biblical background, they were unable to pick up on any of the cross-Biblical allusions within the sermon. Furthermore, these once-per-year visitors are actually looking for tradition rather than innovation. Whether or not it is right to give it to them is another matter!

Alternative approaches

Both the context and the passage lend themselves very well to a narrative approach. A midnight service is certainly not the

twisted into disappointment – another example of multi-layered meaning. In one sense, the narrator is just telling his tale, but in another we must ensure that it is the tale of everyman.

my knees began to yield – deliberately inserted in view of the likely congregation on this occasion. Often on this special night, caught up in the wonder of the moment, many who are distant from God find themselves on the very brink of embracing it all.

And this is mine – we end as we began, with a gruffness on the character's part almost as if he resents having told us the story. That said, his desire for privacy about his feelings towards Christ may reflect that of many of those who listened to him.

place for weighty exposition, and an element of theatre and entertainment is highly appreciated. However, it might have been better to employ a narrative technique which did not necessitate the invention of a supplementary character whose identity was not obvious.

Sermon 4.2
Kindness – Dorcas (Acts 9:32–43)

Context

This sermon was preached as part of a series on the fruit of the Spirit as displayed in the lives of various women in the Bible. Since kindness is a term in such common general use, a narrative approach gave the opportunity to demonstrate it in a human life, rather than to discuss it in any abstract way. A prop was also used on this occasion – a beautiful woven shawl.

Preparation

Read the Word

Since Dorcas appears only in this particular passage, there is no other Biblical material to which we can turn. However, once we read it through several times, a number of things begin to emerge. We notice, for instance, that she has a reputation for kindness within the town, a fact which is emphasised by the degree of mourning among the local widows. How did she earn it? We also notice that Luke draws our attention to her name in both Aramaic and Greek. The number of precise details, while typical of Luke's writing, also emphasises that this was a story which was to be remembered in the faith community and from which the readers were expected to learn.

Read the words

There are numerous details here which should be researched before tackling the narrative. The most important is a map, both to locate the story itself and also to note the distances between the two towns involved. The meanings of the names and the other occurrence of the name Tabitha also repay careful research.

Holy imagination

In this instance, our holy imagination must fill in the blanks about why this person was so popular. What had she done to win such a place in the hearts of the local women – and why did they mourn her so? If the sermon is to meet its aim to put flesh onto the bones of kindness as a concept, such details are vital. In this particular instance, the text demanded that she should be a widow, which meant that I had to invent a husband too!

Supplementary character

Our supplementary character here is a local widow who has been a beneficiary of Dorcas's kindness. She allows us to feel both the benefit of her kindness and the pain of her loss.

Kindness – Dorcas (Acts 9:32–43)

Shhh ... come in. This is a holy place, you see. I've seen God here. Not always of course ... **goodness, no**. We used to come up here with Dorcas. We'd climb up those stairs. Well – we'd climb and we'd joke with Dorcas about bounding up them – what with her name meaning 'gazelle' and everything. She always laughed at that. Then we'd sit up here with the sun pouring in through that window and the sounds of the street below coming in. **Merchants' cries and boys chasing down the street. Sometimes the smell of fish freshly unloaded or spices from the boats**. We would sit here ... and she would listen to our widows' tales – sometimes smiling, sometimes frowning, but always listening. Then it would be time to leave, and Dorcas would hand out gifts – lovely gifts like this shawl here – all made by her.

It's not easy being a widow, **you know**, not round here. You're on your own. And you have to mop up the dregs of other people's charity wherever you find them. It never felt like that with her, mind. She loved to give things, costly things, and expected nothing in return. Nothing. If you ever asked her why, she'd say: 'It's like this new life of mine – all mine for nothing'. We thought she might change when she went religious, called herself a follower of Jesus. We thought she might want nothing more to do with Jewish women like us. But she just went on giving ... and giving ... and giving. So kind. **You always think the best things will last forever, don't you?**

Imagine how we all felt with news that our Dorcas was dead. A fever, some said. Working herself silly for the likes of us, more like. We carried her up here, our dead gazelle. We laid her on the bed and set her clothes just so. **And combed her long, beautiful hair**. It was nice to do something for her. Then her Christian friends

Analysis of Sermon 4.2

Shhh ... come in – this 'confidential' tone establishes a rapport between narrator and listener at the very outset.

goodness, no – phrases like this and **you know** later on are designed to keep the narrative conversational.

Merchants' cries and boys chasing down the street. Sometimes the smell of fish freshly unloaded or spices from the boats – note the use of multiple senses. This helps to ensure the maximum number of contact points with the listener.

You always think the best things will last forever, don't you? – few, if any, in the congregation will disagree with this sentiment. It is one of those phrases which builds a bridge between the then of the story and the now of the sermon.

And combed her long, beautiful hair – an image so intimate that it is almost sensual. When dealing with an abstract topic like 'kindness', it is important to anchor it in real, warm human emotions.

turned up. We were embarrassed. Had we done the right thing? **We didn't know how these things should be done. Not for a ... Christian**. 'Yes, yes', they said, it was all beautifully done, but ...

But what? Peter, a friend of Jesus, was in the next town, they explained. Not two days ago, he had healed a man who was all but dead. Maybe ... 'Go, go!' we **shrieked**. We wanted our Dorcas alive if there was the slightest chance. **Twelve miles the men ran in that heat. Twelve miles they walked back with Peter**. When he arrived, he was kind, this great friend of Jesus. Kind but firm. We were all sent out of the room. And I – I watched through a crack – I just had to see. Kneeling at the bed, he bowed his head and spoke softly to God. Then, turning to Dorcas, he said – **well, you see, I'm not really sure. I'm sure he must have said 'Tabitha cumi', which means 'Up you get, Tabitha'. But, with his back to me, it sounded just like those words of Jesus: 'Talitha cumi' – 'Up you get, little girl – up you get, poppet!'** Maybe that is what he said. She was God's little girl, after all. Like father, like daughter. Kind and generous – and spent on behalf of people like me.

When Peter brought her to the door alive and well and smiling, something inside me melted. I reached out my hand and touched her arm – it was warm under the thin material of her dress. She was really alive. God had smiled on this place. **A good, kind God – the kind I believed in long ago, before my husband was taken so young**. It was as if I'd seen his face in her. Alive – then dead – and now alive again. And God in his kindness had reached me through her.

I must stop talking now. The others will be here in a minute. You see, we worship here now. No – not worship her, of course not. We worship Jesus, **the kindness of God**. And, as we do it, we often think of her.

We didn't know how these things should be done. Not for a ... Christian – this brings in your background and research in a subtle way. Remember that Christianity was a new faith at the time, and many were led to believe that it had secretive rituals unknown to the uninitiated. The uncertainty and mystery stands in marked and deliberate contrast to the warmth of Dorcas's acts – and resurrection.

shrieked – this harsh word jars with the tone of the preceding narrative. This is deliberate – it wakes up the listener to the real desperation felt by the women.

Twelve miles the men ran in that heat. Twelve miles they walked back with Peter – there is no need to make this up when simple Bible background research will reveal it to you. It is a considerable distance on foot in the heat, and shows how great the need was.

well, you see, I'm not really sure. I'm sure he must have said 'Tabitha cumi', which means 'Up you get, Tabitha'. But, with his back to me, it sounded just like those words of Jesus: 'Talitha cumi' – 'Up you get, little girl – up you get, poppet!' – commentaries will reveal the uncertainty about the actual words used, and their possible meanings. Here, it is turned to our advantage, as it reflects the narrator's muffled hearing at the door. Without a heavy explanation, it allows us to think about both possible meanings – the word of command, or the tender coaxing to a child (of God)?

A good, kind God – the kind I believed in long ago, before my husband was taken so young – a reminder that kindness must be seen against the backdrop of life's harsh realities. It is precisely this kind of experience which has severed many from God.

the kindness of God – in this form of narrative shorthand, the intimacy of the story and the vastness of a Biblical theme are moulded into one.

Positive aspects

This sermon had two particular positive outcomes. On the one hand, it did indeed dress up the concept of kindness in human clothes so that we could feel it and appreciate it. On the other hand, it brought out a small episode in the great story of Acts in particularly vivid colours. In this way, it encouraged the listeners to go back and enjoy the story for themselves.

Negative aspects

The subtle word-play concerning the Aramaic words *Tabitha* and *talitha* almost certainly went over the heads of the listeners. While easy enough to appreciate in print, where they can be read and reread, this is not the case in live speech. Also, it demands quite a creative leap to realise that the person talking to us is a member of the fledgling Church whose story Luke describes in Acts.

Alternative approaches

While it was undoubtedly right to take a narrative approach in order to keep this sermon from being dry and theoretical, a first-voice narrative is not the only way. It could just as easily have been told as a description of the events which Luke records in the second voice. Alternatively, Dorcas herself could have told her own story in the first voice, rather like Elijah in Sermon 4.4 below, 'Elijah and the voice'.

Sermon 4.3
Palm Sunday (Luke 19:28–40)
Context

This was preached at a Palm Sunday morning service. On this particular occasion, it was not an all-age congregation. Each character spoke from a different place on the platform in the church, in order to distinguish them. There was a focus in the preparatory and responsive worship on examining our different reactions to Christ.

Preparation

Read the Word

Although the Luke passage is the chosen reading, it is important to read the account of the triumphal entry in all four gospels. The subtle differences and the overlaps build up a composite three-dimensional picture, rather like the two images in a stereo viewer used to do. These different accounts should be thoroughly absorbed before trying to capture the story in a narrative.

Read the words

Bible commentaries reveal important background details here. They tell you, for instance, the numbers of people who regularly arrived in Jerusalem for this celebration. A look at maps and modern photographs of the city will also tell you how crowded it must have been in the narrow streets. These can also provide helpful insights into the reasons why the religious authorities were so offended by Jesus.

Holy imagination

Most of the things people are saying in this narrative are extrapolations of the attitudes described in the accounts of the event. Imagination has been used more in how their voices are put together and in how their attitudes are contrasted.

Supplementary character

The characters used here (including Thomas) are two-dimensional only. This is because, on this occasion, we do not need to know a lot about them and their backgrounds. Instead, in keeping with the purpose of the sermon itself, we want to expose their differing attitudes.

Palm Sunday (Luke 19:28–40)

Crowd

I don't know why I did it – didn't then, don't now. **Don't look at me like that**. You'd have done it too, if you'd been there. The city was heaving – one great mass of squashed-together humanity. There must have been **two, three hundred thousand there**, even days before the feast came to a head. There wasn't much to do except spend money in the bazaars – if you had it. And then that morning, the rumours came running into town. **'Jesus is coming, Jesus is coming, Jesus is coming.'** Of course, we'd all heard of Jesus – who hadn't? Here we were, gathering to celebrate God's great deeds in the past. There he was, acting like God on every street corner. **'The people's messiah!'** Healings, forgiveness, **new legs and eyes for old** – it didn't matter to him. And it wasn't just the decent people either. There was this woman next to me in the crowd – you could smell her before you saw her. **All heady perfume, with bangles**

Analysis of Sermon 4.3

Don't look at me like that – though demanding a good degree of confidence and eye contact from the preacher, this kind of semi-aside helps to establish a rapport between the narrator and the listeners from the outset.

two, three hundred thousand there – Bible background research will reveal that these are exactly the kind of figures which would have been involved. It helps to reinforce the impression of Jerusalem as a hot, crowded, slightly threatening place.

'Jesus is coming, Jesus is coming, Jesus is coming' – a verbal 'Mexican wave', which mimics the action of the rumour passing through the crowd.

'The people's messiah!' – borrowed from Tony Blair's famous description of the late Princess of Wales. This acts as a shorthand for Jesus' huge popularity.

new legs and eyes for old – there is something of the pantomime about this description of Jesus. However, to many among both his supporters and his detractors, he seemed like a showman.

All heady perfume, with bangles and braided hair. No problems guessing why she was in the crowd – all those men with money to spend – it is important to remember that it is among some of the most unworthy people (like this prostitute) that Jesus found the best welcome.

and braided hair. **No problems guessing why she was in the crowd – all those men with money to spend.** But she just looked at me, craned her neck to look out for him and **said softly: 'Thank God he's here'.** And sure enough, there he was. An ordinary man on a **borrowed donkey.** Was that really him? No time to wonder about that. Just then, the place erupted. Some rushed forward to throw their cloaks on the ground. Others took the branches they had in their hands, **the special ones they'd bought for the festival.** They threw them down as well. Or waved them above their heads. And then the singing started down the other end of the street. A temple song – right out here in the bazaar. 'Hosanna! Blessed is the king! Blessed is the one who comes in the name of the Lord! Hosanna!' Of course, we all knew the words, sang it every year on the way up to the temple. But not as if we meant it. Right now, we couldn't help singing it. **Everybody filled their lungs and half-shouted, half-sang it until their throats were raw** – well, almost everybody, anyway.

Disciples

Whatever were they doing? Oh, it was good to see them happy, of course it was. We'd had some pretty rough receptions with Jesus along the way, **believe you me.** Sometimes we were hounded out of villages. Once they even tried to kill him – right on his own doorstep. Other times they would beg him to stay, and he would tell them gently that others needed him too. But this was completely unexpected. We were scared stiff of coming to Jerusalem. It was like – well, waving a red rag in front of a bull. He'd upset the authorities enough out in the sticks. So, coming here was madness – and I told him so. **Still, I couldn't leave him, could I?** Would you? So, I thought we'd come in quietly, just us with him on the donkey. Next thing I know, the street is packed.

said softly: 'Thank God he's here' – this soft description treats her as a person rather than a prostitute, as Jesus himself would have done.

borrowed donkey – basically, this is what the story of fetching the donkey in Bethany is all about. The messiah of God arrives not on a white charger in triumph, nor even on his own donkey – but on one that he borrowed.

the special ones they'd bought for the festival – even though a sermon is in the narrative form, it can still be just as instructive as other kinds of preaching. The palm branches were not naturally growing, but were imported specially for the festival – rather like Christmas trees in December. There is a deeper meaning here too, concerning the unwitting fulfilment of ancient ritual.

Everybody filled their lungs and half-shouted, half-sang it until their throats were raw – in a polite church service, it is important to remember that this was a very raucous, physical event.

believe you me – phrases like this create an intimacy between speaker and listener.

Still, I couldn't leave him, could I? – the perpetual dilemma of the disciple when the going is tough – we struggle to live with him, but we cannot contemplate life without him.

The crowd are going wild. The donkey is missing its footing for branches and cloaks and all sorts. And to crown it all, they start singing. Hundreds of them joining their rough voices in one great song. 'Hosanna! Blessed is he who comes in the name of the Lord!' What did they have to go and sing that for? The sound **bounced around** the narrow street, echoing off the walls and houses, doubling the sound. Goodness knows what the Pharisees would think.

Pharisee

I'll tell you what this Pharisee thought, **Thomas**. I thought it was **the end**. When a man turns water into wine … when a man brings children back from the grave … when he starts to forgive prostitutes and accept homage … when he speaks with the **authority of heaven in the language of the marketplace** … when he calls God 'Father' and sounds as if he means it – it's the end. The waiting is over, the promises are kept. And people like me aren't needed any more. So what did I do? **I signed his death warrant, of course**.

Analysis

Positive aspects

The advantage of setting out the story in this way was that it emphasised in the strongest possible way the difference between the attitudes of the characters. They were separated both by space and by voice. By focusing on just three voices from the thousands of people in the crowds, it made the whole thing personal – which was its aim. Many enjoyed this as a sensory, rather than a theoretical, treatment of the subject.

The crowd are going wild – the switch to the present tense creates a jolt of immediacy, especially useful in first-voice narrative.

bounced around – a visual image for an auditory event – this mixing of the senses can make for a richer narrative experience.

Thomas – this identifies the foregoing disciple, with his qualms and doubts. By naming him, the whole narrative becomes personal, and Thomas stands out as a three-dimensional character.

the end – these two words work on more than one level. The Pharisee himself hopes that this will indeed be the end of Christ's popular reign. The listener, on the other hand, knows that these events signalled the beginning of the end for the Pharisees and their era.

authority of heaven in the language of the marketplace – this lies at the heart of the establishment's unease with Jesus.

I signed his death warrant, of course – a very stark ending, but it leaves the question hanging in the air as to how we react to the threat and challenge of Jesus.

Negative aspects

Some listeners found the contrast between the characters, even when separated spatially, hard to follow. For others, the three characters were almost too interesting, and detracted from the overall purpose of examining attitudes to Christ.

Alternative approaches

It is perfectly possible to preach on this in a more traditional propositional manner. By referring to the text itself, and other supporting texts, a good case can be drawn up surrounding the different attitudes to Jesus expressed on Palm Sunday. From there, a skilful preacher can draw a connection with the attitudes in the contemporary congregation. Alternatively, the whole thing could have been preached as a first-person narrative by one supplementary character observing the attitudes of the three groups.

Sermon 4.4
Elijah and the voice (1 Kings 19)

Context

This sermon was preached as part of a morning-and-evening series on different aspects of Christian life. On each occasion, a given topic was looked at in a thematic way in the morning and then examined in the life of a particular Bible character in the evening. On this occasion, the theme was guidance – examined in the morning and demonstrated in the evening. The congregation were of different ages and mainly regular churchgoers.

Preparation

Read the Word

One of the most important elements in preparing this narrative was a repeated reading of Elijah's story – from beginning to end. This runs right the way from his initial call to his final departure into heaven on the flaming chariot. It is only in this way that you can start to develop a feel for the man and his emotions.

Read the words

Biblical background material can help to understand many elements of the story here. It can explain the failings of the king and the dominance of his wife. It can also cast some light on the peculiar practice of the prophets of Baal as they cry out and cut themselves. Maps and photographs can also give a feel for the distances involved – and of quite how isolated Elijah was on Mount Horeb.

Holy imagination

While it is obvious that no supplementary character is necessary here, a lot of imagination has gone into the creation of Elijah's character. It was important to emphasise his (well-documented) ambivalence about his role, and the mixed blessings he found in hearing God so clearly. Imagination has also been used to provide rhythm and texture within the narrative.

Elijah and the voice (1 Kings 19)

I liked Elisha – bright boy, full of promise. Not a boy really, but he seemed like it to me back then. He was so keen, so wide-eyed, so **'up for it' as you would say today**. Of course he got my back up on that first day, wanting to run off and 'tell mummy and daddy', but that was soon forgotten. We became the best of friends, he and I. By the time the end came, he wouldn't take his eyes off me. I tried to go to Bethel, and he came to Bethel. **I tried to go to Jericho, and he came to Jericho. I tried to go to the Jordan, and he came to the Jordan**. He was sticking to me like glue, no matter what. When the time came to part, and he asked me for a double portion of God's spirit, I could have hit him. 'Silly boy, it will kill you like it nearly killed me.'

But what could I do? I couldn't refuse him, couldn't refuse to leave him either. I was under orders, like I had been from the start.

And what a start. **'Elijah the Tishbite'** – not a very prepossessing start for a prophet, is it? A nobody from the back of nowhere, doing nothing in particular. One day poverty, obscurity and grime – **the dust of the earth in my hair and in between my toes as I tilled it**. Next day, my bare feet padding across the king's **marble floor**, leaving a trail like a cat with muddy paws. His wife was the real cat though, looking at me from beside the throne like **she would torment me and kill me, slowly, just for the pleasure of it**.

'No rain king.' That's how it came out – like a heavenly telegram with no full stops. But that's all I had to say. 'No rain king, not for three years.'

Then I left. Thank God for **the voice** when it came. 'Run, Elijah. Go now, up into the mountains. Hide yourself in the hills – the birds will feed you.' It's surprising how quickly the bizarre

Analysis of Sermon 4.4

I liked Elisha – bright boy – the use of the diminutive term 'softens' Elijah a little. If he is to be our guide through this sermon, we must feel that he is approachable.

'up for it' as you would say today – one of numerous bridges between the then of the story and the now of the sermon.

I tried to go to Jericho, and he came to Jericho. I tried to go to the Jordan, and he came to the Jordan – the use of rhythm is very important in this sermon: it helps to retain drama and pace.

'Elijah the Tishbite' – this epithet for Elijah, drawn straight from scripture, epitomises his humble and unprepossessing beginnings. There is an air of self-deprecation in his own use of the term.

the dust of the earth in my hair and in between my toes as I tilled – the use of as many senses as possible is important in the telling of the story.

marble floor – the kind of detail which can be picked up from Bible commentaries.

she would torment me and kill me, slowly, just for the pleasure of it – this acts as a kind of shorthand, summarising all that we could learn about Jezebel from here and elsewhere in the Bible.

'No rain king.' – this ungrammatical phrase reflects Elijah's nerves and emotion at this first prophetic encounter. Like many prophets, he needed to 'grow into' his voice.

the voice – this phrase is repeated as a kind of leitmotif throughout the sermon. In the end, the listener will be asked to reflect on his or her relationship with the voice of God.

becomes routine. **Day followed day** in the ravine with the crags towering over me. Each morning would bring the sound of approaching wingbeats. Dark shapes in the sky would take the form of birds – **black shiny ravens with gimlet eyes and gnarled feet**. A piece of bread from one and a lump of meat from another, then they would spread their wings and fly off into the sunrise – or the dusk. I would sit and chew on the bread as the meat **crackled** on the fire. I would turn the bread over in my mouth and wonder if it tasted like **Moses' manna of old**. He was out on a limb too – a foolishly brave hero. A man led to the brink by **the voice**.

And then it came again – the voice with my marching orders. First to Zarephath – a sad woman with a generous heart. **The voice**, bringing life where there was death.

Three long years ticked by, until the voice broke the silence. Time for rain, and time for me to confront the king again. I sent for him this time. **My, how I had changed!** The voice had transformed my own. Sure enough, his servant fetched him and he came out to meet me – **a shabby king in a shabby land**, dust flying up under every royal footstep. 'You troubler of Israel', he croaked. 'Not my trouble, sire, but yours. And there's more where that came from.' (What was I saying?) 'Bring the prophets, let them come. Bring those **flunky prophets** of your wife's too. Let them come up to the mountain, and we'll soon see who makes the trouble round here.'

Thud, thud, thud went the drums. Every beat reverberated round my head as their dancing feet ground the hillside into a pulp. Thud, thud, thud. 950 of them – you could smell the sweat on their bodies after hours of the endless chanting. Thud, thud, thud. Then the knives came out – blades glinting in the midday sun. Some cried out as steel met flesh. Others swooned, and

Day followed day – rhythm.

black shiny ravens with gimlet eyes and gnarled feet – it is important not to oversentimentalise a familiar story such as this one. In fact, this is quite a disturbing image, with echoes of Hitchcock's *The Birds*. Elijah's time of isolation must have been lonely and strange for him.

crackled – an onomatopoeic word after so many visual ones. The aim is to invoke and not just describe.

Moses' manna of old – a shorthand to link this story into the overarching Biblical narrative.

My, how I had changed! – in this phrase, our first-person narrator almost stands outside the story, commenting on how much has changed since his prophetic ministry began. It is quite possible to see this growing confidence as we read the Bible story.

a shabby king in a shabby land – 'shabby' is a particularly evocative word, evoking not only the king's physical appearance but also Elijah's feelings about him.

flunky prophets – here, few words are used to convey a lot of information. Commentaries tell us that these prophets were under the direct, and malign, influence of the queen.

Thud, thud, thud – as the pace quickens and the drama heightens, this use of rhythm is even more important.

others staggered on in their mindless circle. Round and round and round.

'Enough!' I cried. My voice sounded strong enough, but it felt like the squeak from my throat on that first day in the throne room. Then I took charge, as much to quell my quaking as to get their attention. Some heaved the heavy stones back into place to rebuild the altar of the Lord. Others fetched water – jugs, pails, pitchers, barrels, anything they could find, until the air itself reeked with the smell of damp timber.

'Now Lord, speak.' I prayed to the cloudless sky. Praying, yearning for the voice to come again so they could hear it. Not for my benefit this time, but theirs – these common, hungry, misguided people. They can hear it, can't they?

CRACK. The whole air ripped apart as the fire fell. Altar, stones, timber, grass, mud – all turned to vapour in an instant. Then everything descended into a kind of chaos. **Death cries from some and anger from others. Triumph and terror. All that mopping up as the rain began to fall. Bloody water in the chariot tracks all the way to the palace.**

'Enough', I muttered, and slunk away into the desert. 'Enough', I pleaded, and climbed away up the mountain. For the first time ever, I wanted the voice to stop. No more voice. No more marching orders. No more heavenly road signs. **No more Elijah the Tishbite.** And then it came. The wind roaring past me, tossing boulders down the mountain like children's toys. The earth itself quaking as if everything would break. The very rocks crackling and sizzling under the flames of God. Then, a whisper, softer than a stolen kiss. **A brush with eternity, gentler than a butterfly's wings.** And that's where Elisha came in – silly boy, wearing my cloak.

Now here I stand on a mountain again. Moses is here too – Moses! The brave voice in the wilderness. And Jesus too – radiant

Death cries from some and anger from others. Triumph and terror. All that mopping up as the rain began to fall – staccato phrases rather than sentences, thereby reflecting Elijah's anguish and emotion at this terrible moment.

Bloody water in the chariot tracks all the way to the palace – the small detail that reflects the big horror, like the girl in the red coat in *Schindler's List*, or the bottle in Nevil Shute's *On the Beach*.

No more Elijah the Tishbite – by repeating this original description, it is as if Elijah longs to return to his roots before such things began to happen.

A brush with eternity, gentler than a butterfly's wings – by transposing an audio experience in the story into a tactile one in the sermon, this jolts the listener out of overfamiliarity.

Now here I stand on a mountain again – in one phrase, centuries of Biblical history are crossed, and we find ourselves in the New Testament on the Mount of Transfiguration.

Jesus. The voice in a human throat. God's smile in human eyes. Down there, I see others. Peter, James, John, decent people with hopeful faces, waiting to hear the voice. And further down still, I can pick out others – **John, Stephen, Sally, Colin, Richard** – bags packed and ready for the off. They are waiting for the voice too.

Waiting?

Positive aspects

This was the first narrative sermon I ever preached, and therefore the congregation weren't expecting it. For some, this brought new life to an old and familiar story, while others were positively disturbed by it. Interestingly, it was the newer Christians, both in age and in years of Christian experience, who warmed to it the most. One younger Christian commented that he liked it particularly because it 'didn't tell him what to think and left him with work to do'.

Negative aspects

Chapter 8 will look at the need to introduce this style gradually and carefully to a congregation. Some of the lessons discussed there were learnt while preaching this sermon! The sheer novelty of the style meant that some were still adapting to the approach by the time the sermon was nearing its end. This also meant that some struggled with the device towards the end of placing Elijah on the Mount of Transfiguration.

Alternative approaches

I have no doubt that narrative offers a particularly vivid way of tackling this subject matter. Especially in contrast to the more propositional approach taken in the morning service, it provided

John, Stephen, Sally, Colin, Richard – these were the names of real people in the congregation, intended as a reminder that they have as much importance and access to God as Elijah did.

Waiting? – the question is left hanging, in order to positively disturb. Will they listen or not? Are they awaiting God's instructions or not?

a good counterpoint. However, it could be tackled using a third-voice narrative, as discussed in Chapter 6. This would have retained much of the impact but increased the application.

Sermon 4.5
Easter voices (John 19:38–20:17; Matthew 28:11–15)

Context

This sermon was preached at the end of a very busy Passion week, at a quiet and reflective evening service. Chairs were placed in the round, and there was an overall informal atmosphere. The aim was to experience, in this more intimate context, some of the personal impact of the Easter story. The spice-seller's story was in fact read out by a female member of the congregation.

Preparation

Read the Word

As with some of the Palm Sunday narrative above, this sermon required a reading of all the Gospel accounts of the resurrection. Each of them picks up on different elements of the story and then reflects back on the feelings which must have been experienced by the key players.

Read the words

Biblical background material is vital here for the sense of authenticity. What were the spices placed on the body? What did they taste and feel like? Who was in the Roman army, and how did they feel about it? Research about the layout of the garden and the look of the tomb can help to fix it in your mind too.

Holy imagination

A lot of imagination has been used here, not only in the creation of the characters but also in contriving the interweaving of their stories. In order to make the narrative function, we have Nicodemus buying his own spices, Joseph of Arimathea helping to deliver Christ's body himself to the garden, and a conveniently placed gardener! Not only this, but also it has been necessary to create a house of some splendour for the soldier. This bolsters his image as a man who has 'got rich quick' through dishonest gain. All these things allow the narratives to work as a three-part story.

Supplementary characters

The lead characters in the Easter story are so well known that it was a distinct advantage to invent others on this occasion. Thus, for instance, we can observe Nicodemus' love for his Lord from a discreet distance, and we can stand with the gardener in the trees and watch Mary's reunion with her Lord. This actually gives us more rather than less facility to examine the emotions generated by these momentous events.

Easter voices
(John 19:38–20:17; Matthew 28:11–15)

The spice-seller

In my job, I get to meet all sorts of people – all sorts.

I meet fearful cooks – skilful women, but **afraid of their master's beating**. They come here and pore over my spices, begging me to tell them what their masters want to tickle their Roman palates. I don't know really. But over the years I've picked up hints from those who do. So I try to suggest a pinch of this and a sprinkle of that and they go away happy.

Then there are the Roman priests. They swish up to my stall as if I ought to quake before them – and I never do. Inside, my skin crawls with loathing for **them and their dark arts**. But instead I smile and smile. Their money cheapens me, but it's too late and I have too little pride to turn it away.

The best customers, or the richest at least, are the widows. They come to me, swathed in their mourning robes and speaking quietly, as if they might disturb the dead if voices were raised. They'll spend hours picking up the **little bottles of aloe and myrrh** – ointments for a dead husband. Sometimes they'll pour a drop or two of the **sticky resin** out on their fingers, rub them together and then breathe deeply of the sickly scent. What are they looking for, I wonder? Some of them are lavishing the care on their man in death that he never had in life. Spending his money, and saving plenty still for later, they are salving their consciences as they anoint his body.

Death and life, meals and burials – it's all part of the job.

But I'll never forget the day Nicodemus came to my stall. I have never, never had a member of the Jewish Council come to me. The great men have lesser men to do their shopping for them.

Analysis of Sermon 4.5

afraid of their master's beating – in order to establish a rapport with the character, there is something conspiratorial about phrases like this.

them and their dark arts – like many today who are not truly Christian, but who bridle at the occult.

little bottles of aloe and myrrh ... sticky resin – the result of careful research about the types of spices. With good Bible handbooks, there is no reason why such details should not be authentic.

Stale Bread?

When he stood before me, my first response was to lower my eyes respectfully to the ground. But when I raised them, guess what I saw? There were tears in them – tears in the eyes of the great man himself! In a quiet voice, deep with authority but fractured by grief, he told me what he wanted. Aloes, the finest I could offer, and **myrrh – the oil of kings**. He wanted enough to embalm a body properly – with not a pore of the precious skin left uncovered. Now, I don't know why I did it. I've never done it before and I'll never do it again. It's an unforgivable intrusion on the hallowed ground of grief. But I asked him outright who it was for. At that, he smiled, actually smiled. And this is what he said: **'It's for the Messiah – I want to anoint the anointed one'**.

Secretly, shamefully, I followed him when he left. I'm not a good Jew. In fact, I'm a bad one. No good Jew would sell spices to the Roman priests or pander to our pagan masters. But I'm still a Jew. And if the Messiah is to be buried in my lifetime, I thought – I want to see it. I followed him right to the edge of Gethsemane, saw which tomb he was headed for, and resolved to come back the next day and see for myself. As I slipped from the garden, **a rich man, one of our great leaders** here in God's city, came in with servants bearing a body under its shroud. Death comes to all in the end.

The next day I rose early, washed the lingering scent of spices **from my hair and my nails. It felt like going to a sacred place** – like the temple but better. When I got there, I entered directly through the gate and headed for the tomb. The air was crisp and new – **crackling with some sort of energy** as if it were the world's first morning. The tomb, when I got there … was empty. Grave clothes tossed aside, the scent of my spices heavy in the air – but empty still.

myrrh – the oil of kings – one of the advantages about using the first voice is that one can introduce comments with a depth of which the character is unaware – such as her unwitting reference to the Kingship of Christ here.

'It's for the Messiah – I want to anoint the anointed one' – in a subtle way, the listeners are reminded here about the actual meaning of a very familiar term – Messiah.

a rich man, one of our great leaders here – this is actually a reference to Joseph of Arimathea bringing in the body of Jesus. Only the sharpest of listeners would pick this up, but it helps to hold the narrative together.

It felt like going to a sacred place – once again, this operates on many levels. The listener knows that it is indeed a sacred place, but she is unaware of that.

crackling with some sort of energy – both this and the images in the next narrative suggest that something freakish is happening here. When the physical laws of the universe are overturned, we must expect many strange things to happen – like the dead walking from their tombs in Matthew's gospel.

Stale Bread?

The gardener

I make it my business not to disturb the visitors here. I tend this garden lovingly for the dead who sleep here **awaiting their call**. But it's the living you need to look out for. Their grief makes them fragile, like the thinnest china. Or sometimes it turns them inside out and makes them angry. I've seen the quietest man shouting at these ancient olive trees until their leaves shook and rustled. I've seen young women go from tears and sighs one minute to vicious outbursts the next – blaming the gods, blaming their children, even blaming me, the gardener.

So, when the young woman fled away on that Sunday morning, I was hesitant to approach her. I could see the grave behind her, **its mouth yawning** open like a wide 'O' of surprise. Of her face I could see nothing. Her hands were clasped to her face, and her veil flapped and wrapped around her as she ran.

Then she stopped and looked up. Her face was beautiful, her lips full, her cheekbones high. Many a man had drowned in those almond eyes, I'm sure. They glistened now with tears – as fresh as the dew on the grass. But all around was the raw red of a night spent weeping. I know the signs, I've seen them often enough.

'Gardener', she said. 'This is your place. You rule here, respecting the beds of the dead and tending the paths for the living. You see many come and go. What have they done with my Lord?' Her voice **cracked and broke up**, as if crumbling under the weight of her emotion, and she threw her arm back in a hopeless gesture towards the chilly, empty grave.

As I parted my lips and cleared my throat to speak, another voice answered her. It was not me she was talking to after all. There, behind me, was a man. Now, I don't want you to think the wrong thing, and these calloused hands will be swift to put you right if

awaiting their call – there is room, even in a first-person narrative, for good Biblical research. This phrase reflects Jewish belief at the time that the dead were awaiting their summons to God's side.

its mouth yawning – a somewhat disturbing image, evoking both caves and traditional dramatic depictions of hell. For all those directly involved, the events of Easter morning were deeply unnerving at first until they understood them.

cracked and broke up – it's important that we feel the raw emotion of Mary here.

you do. But he was a beautiful man. His skin seemed to **absorb the sparkle** of every drop of dew and bounce it back again. His eyes seemed to reflect not only the brightness of the morning sun but also the mellow depth of the setting sun. His voice seemed to carry at once the music of the waking birds and the creak of the ancient trees. It sounded … like the voice of God.

'Mary', he said, and the young woman rushed past me and flung herself at his feet, worshipping the very ground on which he stood. 'My teacher', she replied. The rest was lost as I turned away. This was a private moment, **like a soldier coming home from the war** into the arms of his wife, or a lover meeting her lost soulmate. But I'll tell you something – I wanted to listen, I really did. I wanted him to talk to me, to give me his full attention, to tell me that all was well – and better than it had ever been.

And I'll tell you something else. Yesterday, I stole a glance at the body of that young man as they laid it in the tomb that's empty now. It was a terrible mess – all congealed blood and broken bones. But as sure as I'm standing here now – it's the same man who spoke to that young woman the next day. Has the world gone mad, or have I found my sanity?

The get-rich-quick man

See that smile? That's the sweet smile of success, **that is**. And I'll tell you what – no-one, but no-one is going to wipe it off my face.

I've tried being down, and I didn't like it. When the Romans came into this city with their glinting spears and their pagan symbols, **I was first in line** to join their army. I stood there meekly waiting my turn. I took the oath, the sacrament of allegiance to the emperor. When the centurion **clasped my hands between his meaty fists** and made me repeat the words, I could smell the

absorb the sparkle – these images attempt to convey the sense of magnetism about the risen Christ which is suggested by the Gospel accounts of Mary's rush to touch him.

like a soldier coming home from the war – here there is an irony, since the listener is aware that Christ has, in some sense, returned victorious from a battle.

that is – as with the previous character, little interjections like this help to establish an early rapport with the character.

I was first in line – this unseemly enthusiasm to serve the occupying army tells us something about the character straight away.

clasped my hands between his meaty fists – research in Bible encyclopaedias and dictionaries will tell you about the oath or 'sacramentum' sworn by a recruit to the Roman army. Placing his hands between those of his commanding officer, the new recruit would swear allegiance to the Emperor unto death.

oil and garlic on his breath. But I did it. I wanted work, and I was prepared to do whatever it took to get it.

It wasn't glamorous when it came, believe me. Sometimes it was the punishment detail – accompanying some poor wretch on his way to the cross. When I first started, I would feel sorry for them – **their rags soiled in their terror and their wrists chafed by the rope** as they walked and stumbled and fell. But soon it became just another lousy part of the lousy job. If anything, it was a game – seeing if you could make them squirm that little bit more on their final walk.

Then came the last duty of all – **my making and my undoing**. Now, I'm no great soldier. I'm hardly Hannibal with his conquering troops. But guarding a dead man? A child could have done it. It was a joke. Until the early hours it was, anyway. All of a sudden, the world went mad. The ground itself began to shimmer and wobble beneath us. The sky went searing white then dark again, and the other guard and I fell to the ground like a **child's toppled tower of bricks**. I've no idea how long we lay there quivering.

By the time morning came, we were hauled up before the holy men and made to tell our story **over and over and over again**. Every time we told it, a little more colour would drain from their faces. Then they would scuttle away to the corner like a bunch of girls frightened by a spider. In the end, they came back and told us they would make a deal. A deal – here in the house of God? **Shame on them! God's money for our silence**. Not even our silence, as it turns out – rather some silly story about 'scary men' coming and stealing the body in the night.

Do you think my pride is wounded to say such a thing? Do you think I care? I live here in my lovely house, with my fountain in the courtyard and my servants to bring me food. Do you think I care about reputation?

their rags soiled in their terror and their wrists chafed by the rope – an extremely unpleasant image ... for an extremely unpleasant event.

my making and my undoing – rather like the spice-seller, the character himself may not be aware of how true his words are.

child's toppled tower of bricks – a particularly domestic image for such a rough person. The deliberate contrast emphasises his terror and his vulnerability.

over and over and over again – the repetition adds to the drama of the moment.

Shame on them! God's money for our silence – there is something very hypocritical about him accusing them of double standards – as there often is with those who accuse the Church of wrongdoing!

I'll tell you one thing, though. Whatever happened that night was **not of this world**. Someone nicked the body – and it wasn't me and it wasn't them. I used to think I was scared of my centurion – a rough bully with scars on his arms and an attitude in his head. But I'm a whole lot more scared of the man who was in that tomb. If I ever have to stand before him and tell him where I got my riches, I'll crumple like those wretches I used to crucify. It's not going to happen though, is it? **Another twenty years and everyone will have forgotten about him.**

Analysis

Positive aspects

The informal context of this service allowed this three-part sermon to work very well. In the less formal setting, the eye-witness accounts had a helpful immediacy to them. Also, the unexpected intimacy led people away from the grand themes of Easter and into a contemplation of their personal response to the story.

Negative aspects

There are two risks associated with taking such a radical approach on such a key day in the Christian calendar. One is that your own people expect a traditional sermon on such an occasion, and the other is that the congregation may include guests who have not been informed about the reasons for narrative preaching as your own congregation have been. In fact, there were a number of guests present on this occasion, although most seemed to enjoy the approach.

not of this world – even this rough character is aware that the Easter events constitute an interruption to the laws of the universe.

Another twenty years and everyone will have forgotten about him – this last phrase was left hanging in the air at a service where Christians had gathered to worship Jesus some 2,006 years later. The irony is deliberate.

Alternative approaches

The interaction of these characters with Jesus in his burial and resurrection could have been examined in a more detached, textually analytical sermon. Alternatively, a narrative approach could still have been used, but employing the second voice. If this were the case, it would probably be better only to describe the events in and around the garden on Easter morning itself.

First-voice narrative: a summary

First-voice narrative can introduce us to a gallery of characters who think, talk and feel as we do. In this way, the gap between Biblical world and contemporary setting is greatly reduced. This can have benefits during the sermon, and also afterwards as listeners return to their Bibles with renewed curiosity. You will probably find that you never read these Bible stories the same way again either! First-voice narratives demand research, confidence and maybe even daring – but their rewards can be great.

Chapter 5

Preaching with the second voice

'Once upon a time.' How does that phrase make you *feel*? Close your eyes, and repeat the words again. Where are you now? Perhaps you find yourself sitting on the carpet in the story corner of your first school. There's a warm glow as you anticipate the end of the day and a return to the comforts of home. Alternatively, it might be the end of the day already, and 'once upon a time' signals the start of a bedtime story, filling your mind with the wonders and mysteries of which dreams are made. Maybe you associate those words with a special person who would take the time to tell you stories in your formative years. Of course, stories play a part in our lives long after childhood is over. Dreamworks, the makers of the phenomenally successful *Shrek* movies, have certainly recognised that children of all ages like to be told stories! That, however, is just the point. We like to be told stories ... which implies a teller. In his analysis of the archetypal fairy story, Bruno Bettelheim says that 'To attain to the full its consoling properties, its symbolic meaning and most of all its interpersonal meanings, a fairy tale should be told rather than read' (from *The Uses of Enchantment*, copyright © 1975, 1976 Bruno Bettelheim).

Of course, there is more than one way to tell a story. Sometimes, as we have seen in Chapter 4, it can be told by the person at its heart. This is known as a first-voice narrative. A story told in the first voice has an immediacy, a breathless excitement that is hard to ignore. When a person describes an experience or an event by saying 'I was there', it calls out for our attention. However, by taking a step back and describing it from a narrator's point of view, we create an altogether different feel. This is known as a second-voice narrative, and has particular benefits.

Benefits of using the second voice

Familiarity

If we are going to listen to a story, in the main we expect a narrator to tell it to us. Since this has been the case almost as long as stories have been told, it means that using a narrator has a helpfully familiar ring to it. We are attuned to listen to stories in this way. Jane Austen makes use of this in what is surely one of the most famous opening lines in English literature:

> It is a truth universally acknowledged, that a single man in posses-sion of a good fortune must be in want of a wife. (*Pride and Prejudice*, 1796)

The reassuring familiarity of the narrator's voice allows us to relax and enjoy the content of what follows. Others, from crime writers and romantic novelists through to Alexander McCall Smith with his evocative descriptions of Botswana, have followed in similar vein. The voice of the narrator becomes our companion on the journey, introducing us to a new world of characters, experiences and emotions.

While the preacher often has a role to play in overturning convention and challenging expectations, there are other times when it is wise to work within them. If a communication tool has been proved to work by some of the world's greatest communicators, we should not be afraid to press it into service in preaching. As William Booth *almost* said, 'why should the Devil have all the good stories?'

Commentary

Unlike an eye-witness, the second-voice narrator can comment upon the story. Their position allows them to reflect on feelings, emotions, doubts and possibilities in a way which the first-voice narrator cannot. When it comes to preaching, these things would be out of place in a straightforward exposition, and would seem overly contrived in the mouth of a first-voice narrative. However, in the second voice, we expect to hear such things. We expect to hear not only about what a character is doing but also about how they are feeling, what they are afraid of, and where their actions may lead them. As a narrator, you can choose your vantage point from which to tell the story. Think, for a moment, about a depiction of the crucifixion. We could observe it from the distance, with the three crosses silhouetted against an angry sky. Alternatively, we could place ourselves among the crowd at the foot of the cross. We could even look directly up into the face of Jesus above us. In fact, a skilful narrator can alternate between these perspectives for the sake of emphasis, like a television camera zooming in for the close-up after setting the scene.

We see an example of this in Sermon 5.1 below, 'Love – the dinner guest'. The sermon describes the encounter between Jesus and the sinful woman at Simon's house in Luke 7:36–50. In it, the narrator chooses to move rapidly from a general view of 'the looks on the faces of Simon's guests' one minute to a tiny detail of the grapes on the table, 'their skins bursting with juice as they caught the evening sun' the next. Such variation in tone and viewpoint keeps the narrative interesting and infuses the sermon with energy.

Interpretation

This brings us onto a timely reminder that the whole exercise is one of preaching and not simply storytelling. A preacher using the second voice in narrative preaching is uniquely placed to comment upon the story. These might be comments about the link between this and other parts of the Bible's story, or about the relationship between the story and its contemporary listeners. Sermon 5.3 below, 'The sound of silence', is on Zechariah, based on Luke 1:57–66. In it, you will find references to quiet summer days and children's blankets! These did not exist in the same way in Zechariah's world, but they do in ours. In a few words, the narrator has built a bridge between two worlds. In the same sermon, the narrator refers to 'Moses the lawgiver', thereby telescoping several centuries of Biblical history into one sentence. The narrator is a powerful person, so beware!

Ambiguity

Remember, too, that the role of the preacher is often, but not always, to make things clear. It was not unknown for Jesus to finish one of his stories with a question. We see this, for instance, in the story of the Good Samaritan. Though designed to clarify the question 'who is my neighbour?' (and therefore, who should I love as such?), in fact Jesus finishes with the question 'which one was a neighbour to this man?' On occasions, we might leave a hint of ambiguity, like a cloud of dust thrown up by a passing vehicle, which will settle long after the congregation has gone home. By preaching in the second voice, the preacher can weave questions into the narrative itself.

Drawbacks of using the second voice

Hermeneutical ask

This is, as some might say, 'a big ask'! If you are going to insert into the narrative subtle links with the overall Biblical story, this presupposes a high level of understanding of the story in the first place. It calls for not just a close reading of the passage under consideration but also a good general knowledge of scripture. Hermeneutical decisions which you make in crafting such a sermon will not be obvious, and therefore call for the highest integrity. Things that would be left unsaid in a simple first-person narrative, and passed on as opinion or conjecture using the third voice, will here be woven into the narrative itself. If you are going to do this, you must be prepared to make courageous decisions about interpreting the Bible, like the translator of a popular Bible version might do.

Linguistic dexterity

In this style, your language is being asked to perform two roles instead of one. On the one hand, it is describing the events, while on the other it is giving value judgements upon them. Thus, a first-voice narrator on Elizabeth's story might say: 'I was glad to greet my cousin Mary, and to share these special months with her'. A second voice, however, might introduce other elements: 'A smile played around Elizabeth's lips at this welcome visitor, but as she stepped aside to let her in across the threshold there were other emotions, too ...'. Unlike a third-voice sermon, where (as we shall see in Chapter 6) the preacher can step in and explain, in the second voice you must explain these things within the narrative itself. Description, application and provocative questions must all find their place within the narrative itself in the second voice.

Homiletical honesty

As with the first voice, you must avoid taking liberties with the text any more than you would in a traditional style of preaching. Your congregation might 'forgive' a character speaking in the first voice for a radical or even negative interpretation of events; and in the third voice you can explain an unorthodox point of view. However, in this integrated style, you must have good reasons for all your interpretations, for you will not have a chance within the sermon to explain them. Thus, in Simeon's story, for example, a first-voice narrator might say: 'even as my words finished, I could see their effect on this young woman, and it saddened me'. We do not know if this is how he felt, but we expect a character to express emotions which are not necessarily articulated in the text. However, a second-voice narrator might put it another way: 'No sooner had Simeon finished speaking than he regretted being the bearer of such ill news'. A listener might well ask of you, as narrator/preacher: what gave you the right to interpret it in that way? You will doubtless have your reasons, but make sure you have them marshalled!

Basic techniques for using the second voice

Before we start to examine some second-voice sermons, it will be helpful to outline a few basic techniques. You can then see how they have been used in the sermons which follow. In some cases, you may feel that they have been put to good use, while in others you may feel that they have been altogether ignored! Advice on actual storytelling techniques is given in Chapter 7. What concerns us here is the techniques employed in reading a Biblical text before a narrative is written.

In his stimulating book *360-degree Preaching*, Michael Quicke calls for a return to the medieval monastic principles of *lectio divina*. He identifies these as fourfold principles, as follows:

1. *Lectio*   the reading aloud of the Bible
2. *Meditatio*   visualising the passage through the use of all the senses
3. *Oratio*   concentrating on God in prayer
4. *Contemplatio* awaiting God's revelation.

Any preacher, whether aspiring to preach narratively or not, would do well to follow these techniques honed over the centuries. They emphasise the place of scripture at the heart of the preaching ministry, and remind the preacher of his or her role as a servant and not a master of the Word. A preacher who lacks humility in this regard is a liability both to himself or herself and to the Kingdom.

As you prepare to preach in the second narrative voice, I would encourage you to follow the steps above. However, I would also add the following:

1. Listen

As you read the story, whether aloud or not, listen for any sounds either described or implied in it. Thus, in the story of Simon's dinner guest (Sermon 5.1 below), we have the sound of jewellery jangling and the awkward silence which follows. Also, in the story of Jesus' breakfast on the beach (Sermon 5.2), we have the sound of feet scrunching on gravel. These auditory clues will give life to your narrative. Never miss out on smells, too (or 'olfactory clues' if you prefer!). Remember that smell is one of our most evocative senses. That is why people marketing new houses pump the smell of freshly made bread into the kitchens, and why prison warders in jail sieges fry onions just outside the barricades!

2. Look

Look out for incidental details in the story. While it is important that these remain only incidental in your narrative, they will nonetheless lend a richness to it. In the story of the demoniac, once again, think about his broken chains. Were they round his feet ... or his ankles? Had they chafed him ... or was his skin too tough to be marked by them? Among the Gospel writers, Luke is the most inclined to provide us with such details. You can also find many of them in the historical books of the Old Testament. Since they were recorded for a reason, make sure you use them.

3. Search

Whatever your passage of scripture, whether a parable of Jesus, the account of a miracle or the story of a battle – look for an underlying theme. What is it really about? Is it a story of defeat or a hymn of praise? Does it encourage loyalty or discourage unfaithfulness? If you can summarise the purpose of the passage in one word, you have gone a long way towards finding a theme for your narrative. It is this technique which identified 'anticipation' as the theme for Sermon 5.3, 'The sound of silence', or 'value' for Sermon 6.1, 'The pearl of great price'.

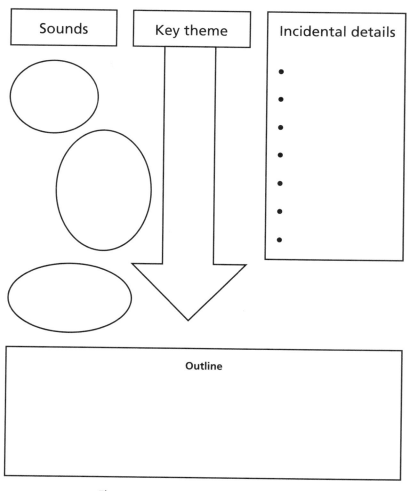

Figure 5.1: *Preparing a second-voice sermon*

You may find that the worksheet (Figure 5.1) helps you with these steps.

Now that we have identified the reasons for using this voice, and the cautions we must exercise, let's look at it in operation.

Sermon 5.1
Love – the dinner guest
(Luke 7:36–50)

Context

This sermon was preached as part of a ten-week series on the subject 'I love God because …'. On this occasion, the narrative style was chosen for two reasons. Firstly, it showed God's love from a different angle. By placing flesh on the theological bones which we all know to be there, it rescued the series from a bias towards the cerebral. Secondly, the congregation on this occasion was an unusual one. The sermon was preached at an ecumenical joint service for all local churches. This provided an opportunity to expose those from many backgrounds to an unfamiliar style of preaching. An initial explanation of the reasons for preaching stories was given, then Luke 7:36–50 was read out, then the sermon was preached. Throughout most of the sermon, I sat on a bar stool with a broken perfume bottle in my hand.

Preparation

Listen

A close reading of the passage revealed a number of sounds. There was the sound of guests chatting over dinner, and the terrible silence when the woman stepped in. From the woman herself, there was the sound of jewellery jangling and the sound of the alabaster jar being opened. There may even have been the sound of her kiss and the soft swish of her hair on the feet of Jesus. There is certainly the sound of muttering among Simon's guests after Jesus has finished speaking.

Look

Since people are reclining at the table, it was clearly a relaxed setting – at least until dinner was interrupted. It is important to note Luke's description of her as having 'lived a sinful life in that town' – since this means that Simon's guests would probably have recognised her. She could not wipe Jesus' feet with her hair unless she broke with convention and loosed it – an important fact in the construction of the narrative. Luke's threefold repetition of 'you did not' will be echoed in the final narrative too.

Search

The underlying theme of the passage is the love of God. In particular, it focuses on our response to that love. Simon clearly knows about the love of God, both as stated of old and as experienced round his table. His problem is that he is so uncomfortable with it. Instead of rejoicing to see it expressed and reciprocated, he finds himself jealous, resentful and even petulant. These kinds of reactions are the ones which the sermon will seek to expose.

Love – the dinner guest (Luke 7:36–50)

Simon liked to think of himself as **broad-minded**. Cutting-edge maybe, as Pharisees go. Oh, his narrow-minded friends would not agree, of course. They wouldn't be seen dead with a freewheeling radical sitting at their table. But, in Simon's book, Jesus was quite a catch. Why, only last week, he had **brought a boy back from the dead**. And now, here he was, sitting at Simon's table. As he looked around, Simon smiled to himself. The looks on the faces of his guests were a picture – a mixture of apprehension and fascination. **What would Jesus do?**

The table did Simon credit. There was **fish**, prepared according to the strictest rabbinic rules, its scent mingling with the rich aroma of **olives**. Here and there were bunches of grapes, their skins bursting with juice as they caught the evening sun. That's when a shadow caught Simon's eye. There it was – crossing the **open courtyard** and falling now over the very shoulders of Jesus. **For a visitor to come in at the end of a meal, asking for pickings from the table, was not unusual.** Even to give them something could be good, just so long as someone was there to see your charity. But NOT NOW and NOT like this. The woman's **jewellery jangled** obscenely as all conversations stopped.

Bending down, **the aroma of her body**, inviting to some and strange to others, seemed to fill the room. And, with a flick of her jewelled wrist, she loosed her hair. Loosed it – here at his table! She might as well have **lifted her dress over her head** and flung it in Simon's lap. HOW DARE SHE! Hardly daring to move his head, he checked the faces of his guests: some appalled, some intrigued, ALL relieved that their table had not been so disgraced. Now a new smell filled the room. It was sweet, heady, almost overpowering.

Analysis of Sermon 5.1

broad-minded – Pharisees receive a lot of bad press, but they were actually astute Biblical scholars. In a country overrun with pagan soldiers, they regarded themselves as the guardians of the nation's spiritual heritage. They may have been arrogant, inflexible and cruel, but they certainly weren't stupid.

brought a boy back from the dead – although we only tend to hear about Jesus' spreading reputation among the common people, we should not assume that the religious establishment was unaware of such an outstanding preacher and healer as Jesus.

What would Jesus do? – the congregation is at an advantage here, because the passage has already been read out. However, a phrase like this is designed to reintroduce the element of tension which is so vital to storytelling. What will Jesus do ... and, for that matter, what will *they* do?

fish . . . olives – chosen both as strongly scented foods, to stimulate the senses of the listener, but also as authentic cuisine for the well-off at the time. It is important that preachers do their homework so that there are not anachronistic references.

open courtyard – again, research in Biblical reference material reveals that people would often dine under a portico, facing onto an open courtyard.

For a visitor to come in at the end of a meal, asking for pickings from the table, was not unusual – rabbinic writings reveal that it was thought good practice to give a visitor leftovers from the table at the end of a meal. This was a charitable act, pleasing to God and impressive to visitors.

jewellery jangled – this alliterative phrase evokes a response in the senses of the listener. It also suggests that the uninvited guest was wearing so much jewellery that it jangled together as she moved. She was a 'painted lady' after all!

the aroma of her body – once again, the senses are stimulated here. The allusion could be to her perfume, or the reference could be more directly sexual. Different listeners will respond to this differently.

lifted her dress over her head – reference to Biblical background reveals that the loosing of hair in public, especially at a Pharisee's dining table, was an extremely provocative act, breaking every social norm. In order to replicate this shock value, the image of her baring her breasts is chosen.

It was perfume. **That woman's perfume**. Trickling down over the feet of Jesus as she wept openly, shamelessly, **cosseting** them with her hair and anointing them. This was appalling. Chin in his hand, Simon could feel the redness creeping into his face, the **sweat gathering in his palms**. His heart beat so loudly that he was sure Jesus could hear it.

'Simon', Jesus said, then began to weave **some story** about a man in debt. At first it was a relief, a distraction. But then Simon had the uncomfortable feeling that Jesus was reading his mind, maybe even writing him into the story. HOW DARE HE! 'Yes, yes', Simon blustered as the story ended. 'Of course the man should forgive.' He was a Pharisee after all, and moral discussions were bread and butter to him. But then he fell silent as Jesus went on talking. Each word seemed to batter on the door of his pride and pretence. Every phrase seemed to **peel something away**, like layers of an onion grafted onto his very flesh.

'You gave me no water.' **Ow!**

'You gave me no kiss of greeting.' **Ow!**

'You gave me no oil of anointing.' **Ow!**

'She is forgiven.' **Ow!**

Long after the guests had gone and the servants had cleared his table, Simon sat in the **dusk**, turning the broken perfume bottle over in his hands. Its scent still stung his **nostrils**, as the words of Jesus stung his heart. If her love was so great because of her forgiveness, why was there so little love in his heart? Shaking his head, **he crushed the remaining fragments of the bottle in his hand**. And let them fall as dust to the ground.

Positive aspects

This sermon has the advantage of arresting language. Its use of all five senses, and the 'misplacement' of shocking images

That woman's perfume – the choice of words evokes the disgust felt by Simon. The perfume of any woman would have been out of place at such a gathering, but with this woman it was particularly unwelcome.

cosseting – hitherto, we have seen the woman only through Simon's shocked and critical eyes. The use of this tender word reminds us that the woman at the heart of the story is enacting her real love and gratitude to Jesus.

sweat gathering in his palms – in contrast to the sweet scent now filling the room, Simon is experiencing a personal hell. This tactile image stimulates another sense for the listener.

some story – to us this is not just *some* story, but *the* story – the point of Luke's story. However, as a 'professional' religious expert, it does not register with Simon as anything special. This hard indifference will recur later. It also echoes the attitude of some listeners who may be overly familiar with Luke's story.

peel something away – the physical image here is both harsh and painful, and deliberately so. The words of Jesus often healed, always challenged, and frequently stung.

Ow! – the repetition of this onomatopoeic word fulfils two functions. Firstly, it evokes the strength with which Simon feels the rebuke. Secondly, it radically alters the pace of the sermon's delivery – thereby ensuring that all in the congregation are still awake. It also evokes Luke's threefold repetition in the story, adding a fourth which then links to the key point of the narrative.

dusk – traditionally a time of quietness and reflection. At this point, after the high drama of the story, it is important that Simon reflects, and the listeners with him.

nostrils – sometimes a spiritual rebuke can be so strong that we feel it with the intensity of a physical sensation. This will evoke challenging memories in the minds of many listeners.

he crushed the remaining fragments of the bottle in his hand – it is quite possible that Simon would have cut his hand badly by doing this, which is deliberate. Like the teenager punching a wall with the express intention of hurting himself, the desire is to deaden emotional pain by replacing it with physical.

like peeling off the dress, ensures that people keep listening. By revealing the emotions seething under the surface of this apparently banal dinner-table setting, it makes the listener consider the story afresh. It also calls to mind the emotions of rejection, anger and shock which can linger round any dinner table!

It also has the advantage of ambiguity. We are made aware of Simon's shock at the intrusion, and his awkwardness at being the focus of Jesus' attention. However, we are left in the dark as to whether Simon ever changed his mind. The sermon does not solve this question, any more than Luke does. The unresolved nature of the story gives it a longer afterlife in the minds of the listeners as they dwell on the unanswered questions. On one occasion when this was preached, the first question asked by a member of the congregation was: 'what happened next?'

Negative aspects

There is a lot of Biblical background which is either assumed or lightly suggested here – the traditions covering loose hair, the nature of rabbinical stories and the tradition of foot-washing to name but three! Using a more traditional approach, these could have been explained more thoroughly. To a modern, Western, demonstrative congregation, the actions of this uninvited guest may seem quite acceptable rather than bizarre. They would be inclined to ask Simon what his problem might be! The absence of explanation leaves the sermon light and lively, but may leave some listeners confused.

Since it is hard to sustain this level of narrative intensity for a long time, the sermon itself is quite short. This means, that within a short timeframe, the preacher must deal with love, forgiveness, tradition, resentment and pride – which is a tall order! However, that said, Luke seems to deal with them in an even shorter time.

Alternative approaches

This story could have been told as a first-person narrative from the point of view of a guest, or the woman, or even Simon himself. Alternatively, it could have been dealt with as a conceptual sermon on the themes of love and forgiveness, with illustrations drawn from the story. The third approach, as we shall see in Chapter 6, is to combine the two – using elements of lyrical narrative and straightforward application.

Sermon 5.2
Breakfast on the beach
(John 21:1–19)

Context

This sermon was preached during the evening service at the end of a Passion Week. During the week, the programme had been packed with studies, meditations, communion services, marches of witness and a musically rich Easter celebration service in the morning. At this quieter service of Easter praise, there was an opportunity to reflect on the ongoing relationship with the risen Jesus, whether for Peter or for us.

Preparation

Listen

There are lots of sounds to note as you read this passage. There is the sound of the water on the sides of the boat and the shores of the lake. There is the sound of the net as it hisses into the water time and time again, maybe with the odd puff of disappointment as it comes back in! Once the fish have been hauled up the beach, there is the crackle of the fire and the spitting as cold water falls on hot coals. Smells abound too – not least the smell of the fire and the fish as it cooks. These will prove very important in Peter's rehabilitation as it is portrayed in the narrative.

Look

There are lots of odd details to look out for here. For a start, there is John's evidence that they have fished all night without catching anything. Put yourself in their position, and you will find that it is not hard to feel frustrated! Then there is the odd fact that John spots Jesus but doesn't go to him, whereas with Peter it is the other way round. Odder still is the way Peter gets dressed *before* plunging into the water, rather than after emerging from it. This would seem to be a mark of respect for his Lord. Notice how John records the exact number of fish caught. The number itself is unlikely to be significant, but it does mean that it was unusual enough for someone to sit down and count them, so that the memory of this event should be preserved for all time.

Search

The key theme here is one of rehabilitation. Peter starts the passage going out onto the lake, as he had done before meeting

Jesus. He ends it following him despite the experiences which have recently scarred him. The focus of the sermon is on the call for the disciple, especially the wounded disciple, to draw close to Jesus and follow him wherever he may lead.

Breakfast on the beach (John 21:1–19)

As the little boat rose and fell, the grey dawn cast an unkind light on Peter's face. Every line was etched deeper, so it seemed. His eyelids were heavy after a night of fruitlessly casting nets into the water. And there was a far-away tiredness inside.

Anger, self-loathing and deep, deep sadness had left scars that years of fishermen's weather could never equal. **The nets, like the man, were empty**.

Even when a stranger called out from the beach, he did not react. Why listen to the voice of a stranger again? A soul prodded too often flinches, **like a frightened cat** hugging the shadows.

But then another voice seemed to rouse him. 'It's the Lord', John said. **John always seemed to know when he was near**, even when no-one expected him. Hardly had he spoken than Peter was heaving himself over the gunwale, sending the boat bobbing crazily as he did so. He began to wade towards the shore **like a man possessed**, his eyes fixed on the figure by the fire.

By the time he clambered out, his coat was wrapped about him, dripping at the hem and **leaving a trail across the stones**. Soon he was sitting by the fire in perfect peace – **like the crazy man** from Gadarea months ago, sitting at Jesus' feet among the tombstones. The **smell of wood smoke** drifted across the beach and out to the boats on the water. It must have stung Peter, though. How many days was it since he had blinked back the wood smoke in the high priest's courtyard, lashing the servant girl with his words as he told her that he knew nothing of Jesus? It could have been a hundred years ago, to see him now.

One word from Jesus about fetching some fish for breakfast, and he was back into the water again. Not one or two, oh no. With his Lord waiting, he took the strain of the whole net which two

Analysis of Sermon 5.2

As the little boat rose and fell – a richly descriptive phrase like this sets a narrative tone straight away, rather like our 'once upon a time' at the start of this chapter. This allows the listener to relax.

The nets, like the man, were empty – in one phrase, this telescopes Peter's recent experiences. It also signals to the listener that the narrative will be dealing not only with observable facts, like the nets, but also with emotions.

like a frightened cat – this is intended to evoke the kind of fear seen in an animal which has been mistreated. A soul assailed or disappointed too often will retreat into a corner like an abused animal, and become spiritually numb.

John always seemed to know when he was near – both within the narrative of the Gospel and in the construction of the Gospel, John shows an uncanny ability to know where Jesus is to be found. With subtle use of language, this kind of teaching can be passed on as readily through narrative preaching as through any other style.

like a man possessed – using this phrase is a high-risk strategy. Although it links with another Biblical story, as we shall see, and also employs a phrase in common parlance, there are considerable risks. The congregation could have been left thinking that Peter actually *was* possessed, which was certainly not the intention!

leaving a trail across the stones – the rapid switch from the distant 'shot' of Peter striding through the water, to the 'close-up' of the drips falling from his hem, keeps the narrative alive.

like the crazy man – here, a link is made with another Biblical story, which can be found in the synoptic Gospels. The parallels in terms of lakeside setting and healing are present but not obvious. I have chosen to emphasise the healing element in this encounter with Peter more than John himself does.

smell of wood smoke – as we have identified above, smell can be one of the most evocative senses. We often link it to particularly strong memories or experiences.

boats had carried between them, its ropes cutting deep into his broad shoulders. He heaved it through the water and up onto the shore, **scrunching** the stones and pebbles as it came. Inside, the mound of fish flapped and thrashed and glistened like living treasure.

Jesus picked some, his hands whole now but **still showing the scars**. For the second time, he took the role of servant – not washing their feet this time, but cooking their breakfast. By now they'd learnt to recognise the King in servant's clothes, and no-one even tried to protest.

Afterwards, with **the smell of fish and bread mingling with the smoke**, and the sun **warming the stones** on the beach, they walked together, leaving the boats by the bulging net. There were more words for Peter now. There are always more words for the men and women he is shaping. He never says 'you're finished now, you're just right'. As long as there are fish to be caught and breakfasts to be cooked. As long as there are **nights of labour with mornings of disappointment**. As long as the acrid smell of failure mingles with the wholesome scent of promise, there will always be more words. Until the fish have swum their last swim. And **until the boats put out to sea no more**. And until the walk on the shore goes on forever without leading you **away from home**. The words will always be the same:

'**Follow me.**'

Positive aspects

After a heavy week in terms of Biblical input, tackling the passage in this way ensured that people connected with it. Its narrative style caused them to relax in such a way that they absorbed its deeper message more easily. The response at the time suggested

scrunching – sounds like these give texture to the narrative, and ensure that it stimulates the listener's senses.

still showing the scars – John himself does not specify that they can be seen, although clearly they can for Thomas in the previous chapter of John's Gospel. Their mention here is to ensure that the listener remembers those events which precede the story.

the smell of fish and bread mingling with the smoke ... warming the stones – there is a mixture of sensory 'clues' here, designed to evoke the scene as powerfully as possible. It is important that the listener is 'kept' with the narrative long enough for it to deliver its theological punch.

nights of labour with mornings of disappointment – clearly, this phrase draws from the imagery in the passage itself. However, the use of the plural builds a subtle bridge to the contemporary experience of the listeners.

until the boats put out to sea no more – we know from elsewhere in the Bible that the Jewish people were afraid of the sea and of the chaos that it represented. That is why the New Earth has 'no sea' (Revelation 21:1).

away from home – the idea of Christian faith as a journey which begins now and continues forever is a recurrent one both in the Bible and in the later history of the Christian Church. This subtle allusion to life after death was an important note to sound on Easter day.

'Follow me' – this final phrase in fact sums up the central thread. The whole sermon is about following Jesus, through thick and thin ... in life and in death. Ultimately, of course, Peter would follow him to a violent death.

that it evoked strong feelings connected with their own initial call to follow Jesus and their ongoing intention to do so.

Negative aspects

The sermon's brevity was a weakness. While the preacher has laboured for hours over the construction of the narrative and its precise choice of words, the congregation hears it only once. Although this creates a very intense impact, it also runs the risk of subtle allusions and careful imagery being overlooked simply because the listeners did not notice them!

Alternative approaches

This could have been presented as a retrospective first-voice narrative by Peter himself. Certainly, this would have allowed for a more candid disclosure of his feelings and disappointments. On this occasion, such an approach was not taken, as a similar approach had been used just two days before at the Good Friday service. Equally, the sermon could have been presented in a much more straightforward way. The preacher could have spoken about Christ's ability to restore our self-esteem, and to follow him regardless. The illustrative material in the story itself would have lent depth and colour to such an approach.

Sermon 5.3
The sound of silence (Luke 1:57–66)

Context

This sermon was preached in the context of a very traditional service of Advent praise. In the lull before the rush of Christmas carol services, it seized the opportunity to focus on a lesser-known part of the story. Set against the backdrop of familiar hymns and readings, it was intended to ask disturbing questions. Also, in a service customarily rich in choral music, it provoked reflection on the use of the voice.

Preparation

Listen

Once again, there are many evocative sounds to listen out for here. There is the unmistakable sound of a newborn baby's cry at the start of the passage. Later on, there is the sound of guests arriving in the house, and Elizabeth's shrill voice drowning them out with her plea that the child should be called John. Think about the sound of Zechariah writing on the tablet with everybody watching him. The most remarkable sound of all would have been his voice. What does a voice sound like when it has not been used for nine months? Does it sound cracked and weakened ... or deep and strong? It is these sounds, alongside the silence inside Zechariah's head, which will form the basis of the narrative.

Look

Look at the relatives and neighbours as they gather around Elizabeth. Look at the shock on their faces as Elizabeth suggests such an unexpected name. It is worth noting, too, that the assembled crowd makes signs to Zechariah in order to get their message across. This tells us that he is deaf as well as dumb.

Search

The underlying theme here is of faith and frustration. Zechariah has endured nine months of (self-imposed) frustration – but both he and Elizabeth must exercise faith over the guidance they have been given. The sermon will focus on the joy that comes from faithful obedience to God.

The sound of silence (Luke 1:57–66)

Whoever said **silence is golden** has not seen a golden death-mask. Perhaps they are thinking of the **silence of a perfect summer's day** in the countryside. Or the gentle, snug silence that settles on the town **like a child's blanket** at the end of a busy day. But they have not known a cruel and spiteful silence. They have not found themselves isolated in a world of shrieks and exclamations and laughter where they cannot join in.

That is where Zechariah had lived **these last nine months**. A terrible silence had descended on him, **suffocating him** as it fell. His voice had gone – his beautiful, deep, cantor's voice. Once upon a time, it had filled the temple court **like the giant wings of a bird** flapping lazily up towards the heavens. Now there was nothing – not a squeak. And the sound of **other people's voices** had gone too. He had lived these past months in a cell with thick, impenetrable, invisible walls. The events of his family were played out before him like a silent movie. He had watched as Elizabeth's womb had swollen **like a ripening fruit**. He had seen, though not

Analysis of Sermon 5.3

silence is golden – this is a deliberately modern phrase. It is intended to assure the listener from the outset that this will have a modern application. It 'shortens the gap' between Zechariah and the listener.

silence of a perfect summer's day – an appealing image, causing the mind to drift to peaceful scenes far away from Advent and Christmas!

like a child's blanket – a deeply evocative image, with echoes of childhood, security and comfort. The juxtaposition of hard and soft, comforting and disturbing images is one of the chief benefits of second-voice narratives.

these last nine months – it is no accident that Zechariah's 'confinement' in a world of silence mirrors his wife's time of confinement.

suffocating him – the application of a physical image to an emotional sensation enhances the impact of Zechariah's suffering.

like the giant wings of a bird – this will be a recurring image throughout the sermon. Often, it is important to create some kind of unifying image which will 'carry' the key message of the sermon.

other people's voices – Luke 1:62 reveals that the family had to make signs to Zechariah in order to communicate. Clearly, he had lost the power of hearing as well as of speech. This kind of careful textual reading is vital in preparing a narrative sermon.

heard, her joy when her cousin Mary came to stay. Theirs was not the only miracle child, it seemed. He had nodded and smiled at the young woman, **like the old fool** he had become.

And now, today, the house was full. There were relatives, whom he knew, and neighbours he hardly recognised. There were faces half-remembered and others better forgotten. And somewhere there, in the midst of them, the face of his son. **HIS SON** – a miraculous little person with a **squidged-up face and ten perfect little toes**. His son. A tear rolled unchecked down his cheek as he thought how much he would love to say those words. After all, this was the great day. This was the day when old Zechariah and old Elizabeth would celebrate like bright young things. Look – there was the priest now. **Bustling** through the door in the robes Zechariah himself had once worn with such pride. Today, the child would be named.

Craning his neck for a better view, his heart missed a beat. Something was wrong. Elizabeth's face was red and cross as she held the child close. Her relatives glowered. What had happened? Things were very animated now – arms waving and fingers wagging. Suddenly, they all stood before him. Some were mouthing strange words, others jabbering as if he could hear. At last, a tablet was produced. On it, the words were scratched: 'What is his name?' With a sigh, he took the tablet in his hand and began to write. **Each letter was slow and deliberate, his wrinkled hands looping around their shapes as if making a work of art**. Around him, every breath was held as he wrote, the only sound made by his hand as it scratched. It was not hard to know what to write. The only voice he had heard for nine long months, waking and sleeping, was the angel's. 'He shall be John … he shall be John.' With a smile tugging at the corner of his lips, Zechariah changed the tense, one small act of defiance. **HE IS JOHN.**

like a ripening fruit – an evocative image as a reminder of the forthcoming baby. Also a reminder that not all sensations were denied to Zechariah – with touch and sight certainly still in working order!

like the old fool – this self-deprecating phrase captures Zechariah's sentiment, and also reflects Biblical reality – by refusing to believe the angels' message, he had made a fool of himself.

HIS SON – repetition can be important in an oral mode like preaching. Unlike in a written text, an important phrase can be missed or forgotten if it is said only once. In a bleak moment, the fact that John is his son is a ray of light to Zechariah.

squidged-up face and ten perfect little toes – these are anachronistic, as they are more modern ways of describing an infant. This is deliberate. Listeners must recognise the emotions if they are to enter into Zechariah's story.

Bustling – the use of all five senses in crafting a narrative is vital, hence this description of the sound of the priest's entry. The word also suggests a degree of gravitas and importance – which Zechariah himself would once have felt in the high priest's role.

Each letter was slow and deliberate, his wrinkled hands looping around their shapes as if making a work of art – from time to time, you should vary the pace of the narrative. In particular, it is important to slow things down and build tension before the climax of the story. The more familiar the story is, the greater the need to create suspense in this way.

HE IS JOHN – in Luke's account, there is a jarring effect as we switch suddenly to the present tense instead of the future. This is replicated in the narrative.

As he handed the tablet back, so it began. At first, it was like the distant rumble of an underground river, strength hidden deep below the surface. Then it grew stronger, like molten lava pounding on the **doors of the earth**, waiting to be released. Finally, it was like the thunder of a hundred horses' hooves, all churning up the dusty ground in unison. Zechariah spoke. Doubt was replaced with certainty. Disbelief with faith. Sadness with joy. And his old, cracked voice found its depths again. **Like a bird long asleep, it spread its wings, shook them and took to the skies**. Every other babbling sound in the house was hushed as his deep and beautiful voice scaled the heights of praise. In a song that seemed as old as **Moses the lawgiver** and as new as tomorrow's unformed dew, he told of the goodness of God. 'The tender mercy of our God, by which the rising sun will come to us from heaven.'

As the song died away and the house began to empty, he murmured soft words to his **little man**, thought about teaching him to sing. He remembered the words of God's rebuke to Moses of old: 'Who gave you your tongue?' And he resolved to use it only for good. **His breath. My voice. His song**.

Positive aspects

One of the key advantages of this sermon was that it gave an opportunity to focus on one of the 'bit parts' in the Christmas story. Zechariah is a man in a position of great spiritual responsibility who makes a bad decision – something with which we are all familiar! The use of lyrical language and striking images allowed the preacher to explore sensitive issues of folly, rejection and isolation without creating an overly heavy tone. When this sermon was preached at a Bible college, one of the students commented that 'today I *heard* the story'.

doors of the earth – this kind of imagery is drawn from elsewhere in the Bible, in particular from the creation passages in Job. This kind of 'internal referencing' builds a familiarity with scripture – particularly important where Biblical knowledge is not high.

Like a bird long asleep, it spread its wings, shook them and took to the skies – here we return to the bird image used before. This kind of repetition gives the narrative artistic integrity, and also provides a vehicle for the key teaching – in this case, the true freedom of the soul when it is yielded to God.

Moses the lawgiver – a concentration on the little stories of scripture can sometimes breed an ignorance of the overall story. This phrase reminds us that both Zechariah and the listener stand on a continuum which stretches back to great men of faith, like Moses.

little man – once again, a contemporary phrase of endearment, in order to shorten the gap between Zechariah and the listeners. After all the anguish which has gone before, this is a moment of touching intimacy.

His breath. My voice. His song – in these six words, the challenge is finally passed onto the listeners. What will they do with their voices?

Negative aspects

Muted response to the sermon at the Advent service may indicate that it was too unconventional or too intense for its listeners. In such a traditional setting, they were maybe expecting a more conventional approach. It is probable that the use of the bird image for Zechariah's voice was 'a bridge too far'. Of course, these things make perfect sense to the preacher, having lived with them throughout the preparation time. The congregation, however, has only one opportunity to hear them.

Alternative approaches

The most obvious alternative would have been to present this as a first-voice narrative by either Zechariah or Elizabeth. This would have brought an immediacy to the narrative and would have allowed a more acute expression of the emotions involved. Alternatively, a third voice could have been introduced, stepping out of the narrative as it stands and applying it. The danger of this, as we shall see in Chapter 6, is that the magic of the moment can be lost, and the sermon's impact can run away like water into sand. Another approach would have been to preach a traditional sermon on the risks of disobedience, with illustrative material drawn from Zechariah's experience.

Sermon 5.4
Simeon and the Word (Luke 2:25–32)

Context

This sermon was preached in an unusual context, in that it was preached for a congregation of preachers in training. It was initially preached at a residential preaching week on narrative preaching, and has since been used at one-day preaching seminars. It is unusual in that it is rare for preachers to hear a sermon about preaching. The focus here is on the relationship between the Word and those who pass it on.

Preparation

Listen

For the most part, we are listening here to unheard sounds. The concentration is on the internal sound of the Word within Simeon's heart and mind. At the same time, there is a rich description of both him and his environment, the temple. This acts like placing the set and the props on a stage ready for the drama to take place.

Look

The incidental details that the Bible gives us about Simeon are fairly minimal. However, we do know that he had been waiting a long time for this. On the day in question, we also know that he was all but propelled into the temple precincts by the Holy Spirit. What might such a person look like ... sound like?

Search

If we look carefully, the underlying theme here is one of faithfully delivering a Word long held in readiness. There is no other example quite like Simeon of waiting carefully and patiently to deliver a Word once sown in the heart by God. For students in training to preach, waiting for 'their big moment', it seemed a particularly appropriate piece.

Simeon and the Word (Luke 2:25–32)

Sometimes he wore it like a crown on his head – a badge of office, attracting envy and admiration wherever he went. Other times, it was more **like a heavy scarf** – cumbersome, but reassuring about his old neck. Other times still, it was like a restless caged bird – **fluttering and battering** itself on the paper-thin walls of his heart. But it was always there. They lived together, these two.

Every day, the two of them would make their way to the temple. In days gone by, he had gone with head held high to play his part. Nowadays there were younger, leaner men to take his place, and he preferred to watch. As many blazing summers had come and gone, so he had grown to know this place like the lines on **his leathery hand**. He knew every cracked flagstone and every scarred brick. He knew where the shadows fell on their daily march around the courtyards. He knew where the poorest would gather to watch without being seen. And where the rich would strut, preening their robes like peacocks for all to see. He knew where the smells of the bazaar would tumble over the temple walls like uninvited guests. And where the **waft of incense** would tug the soul to higher things.

These days he liked to sit, rather than walk, in this hallowed place, and nurse the Word in his heart. It had grown stronger

Analysis of Sermon 5.4

like a heavy scarf – many physical images are associated with the Word in this sermon. This one in particular captures the burden which many preachers feel in handling the Word.

fluttering and battering – this restlessness of the Word of God is something that will be expressed again and again in the course of the sermon.

his leathery hand – it is important to make Simeon as much of a real person as possible. Also, this stresses his great age.

waft of incense – note the use of as many senses as possible in order to engage as many people as possible.

of late, like a bell **on a buoy at sea, clanging insistent in the distance**. Today, it was almost deafening. He could hardly hear a thing above its din by the time they arrived. Their eyes were furtive, this young couple, darting everywhere and clutching the baby's **helpless bundle** tight, as if the whole world depended on it. Feeling that his very head would burst with the noise, he took the child from them and shouted above the clanging Word: 'This is the child!'

And then, in harmony now with the bell's note, he spoke of promises fulfilled and eyes opened, of light shed from heaven and **a sword to pierce the heart** of the young woman who stood before him. Smiling at her, the light dancing in his watery eyes, he returned the child.

It was over now, the waiting done. Simeon returned to the house of his birth. Returned to the arms of his Maker. And the Word, set free from his heart, found its way elsewhere.

In some, it was welcome, like a **stray cat curling up by the hearth** and purring in the background. In others, it was a merciless driver **on their shoulders** – forcing them on over hills and borders, mountains and oceans until they collapsed, spent, at the end of their race. In others still, it was like a mighty **underground river** – kneeling down, you could hear its dull roar, feel its vibrations through the earth itself. And to others it comes still.

Today, the Word rests in your hearts and **scurries** round your minds. Today it **jangles** a merry rhythm on the iron railings of your certainties. Today the sovereign Lord **will not dismiss you in peace**, for your mission is incomplete and the Word must out. The Word shall be flesh as it dwells among you, taking your breath away with its power and giving it back in your weakness.

on a buoy at sea, clanging insistent in the distance – once again, a very physical image for the Word, with echoes of distant and exciting shores, and also a warning about impending danger.

helpless bundle – compared to Simeon, with his age and experience, the baby Jesus is little more than an inanimate bundle at this point.

a sword to pierce the heart – this is a very deliberate reference to Simeon's familiar words in the Gospel itself.

stray cat curling up by the hearth – a cosy image, but nonetheless with a sense that the Word may have come in uninvited.

on their shoulders – a sensation with which many preachers will be familiar.

underground river – wrapped up in those two words are the concepts of both strength and hiddenness.

Today – at this point, the sermon actually slips into the use of the third voice in narrative – a technique which is discussed in Chapter 6.

scurries … jangles – physical images, almost mischievous, suggesting the disturbing power of the Word.

will not dismiss you in peace – a deliberate reversal of the *nunc dimittis* in Simeon's words.

Positive aspects

This sermon gave an opportunity to explore a particular theme with a very particular audience. As any preacher reading this book will know, the opportunities to hear preaching about preaching are few and far between. Furthermore, to do so in a way that was rich in description rather than heavy on analysis was a welcome change.

Negative aspects

While it is never right to extend a sermon for the sake of it, this sermon's brevity was a problem. For those unaccustomed to this particular style, it takes a few minutes to 'tune in'. If the sermon itself is only a few minutes long, it is quite possible to lose some listeners along the way. Also, the reliance on any single image can be a dangerous policy since, if people miss it, they miss out on the central message. Here, the personification of the Word is the one unifying image.

Alternative approaches

This sermon could have been preached in a much more traditional propositional way, examining either the example of Simeon's patience or the content of his prophetic Word. Alternatively, it could have been preached in the narrative style, but from a much more external perspective. This could have been done very effectively with a first-voice narrative description from an invented character, as we have seen in Chapter 4.

Sermon 5.5
Never look back (John 20:10–18)

Context

This sermon was preached on a main Easter Sunday morning service following on from an early-morning communion service. The majority of the congregation were regular churchgoers very familiar with the Easter story. This was the year in which Mel Gibson's controversial film *The Passion of the Christ* was released; and the sermon was preached with a still from the film of a tear-stained Monica Belucci in the role of Mary Magdalene on the screen behind me.

Preparation

Listen

It is quietness that we need to listen out for here – the quietness of the empty garden on the first, dreadful morning after Jesus has died. We can listen, too, for the sounds inside Mary's troubled and weary mind. What else might be heard in the garden – the creak of trees, the sound of birds flying to and fro … or the sound of angelic voices?

Look

There are small details we need to notice here. Everything takes place in the early morning – when man-made sounds are at a minimum and the sounds of nature are loudest. Notice, too, that Mary came to the garden accompanied, but is then left all alone with her thoughts and a strangely empty grave. When she hears the voice of Jesus, it comes from behind, so that she has to turn around for the moment of wonderful revelation.

Search

The underlying theme here is one of transformation. Just as Jesus is transformed from death to life, so Mary is transformed from a weeping mourner to joyful worshipper in an instant. Not only that, but she is transformed from a mere bit part – accompanying the disciples to the tomb ... to a herald of the good news of Christ's resurrection.

Never look back (John 20:10–18)

Just like that, they were gone. The sound of their footsteps faded as they ran from the garden. They had left her ... **like so many men before**. And she was alone. Even though she was the one who had summoned them, blurted out her horror at the **empty, defiled grave**, no-one stayed with her now – there were more important people to tell.

So she was alone, in the stillness of the garden, with her thoughts. They were bad company, her thoughts, always had been. There was a time when they had shrieked and flapped inside her head – beating the insides of her mind and **tearing at it with their outstretched claws**. Then Jesus had clapped his hands, scared them off and sent them flapping away into the far distance. That seemed so long ago now – before the dark night in the city, before the long day at the cross. Now she could **feel them circling again**, just beyond the horizon – eyeing up their prey ... ready to swoop.

Ducking away, she had stolen a look inside the tomb. She was frightened of what she might see. Afraid that the smell of death

Analysis of Sermon 5.5

Just like that – a very sudden beginning. This is to be a very intimate portrait, and is introduced that way from the start.

like so many men before – it seems likely that Mary had led a fairly loose life before her encounter with Christ.

empty, defiled grave – in Mary's cultural setting, the idea of tampering with a body would have been even more distasteful than it is in our own.

tearing at it with their outstretched claws – there are many ways that we could depict demons or dark thoughts. This image of the birds is particularly unnerving, and also allows us to 'convert' it to a positive image at the close of the narrative.

feel them circling again – any listeners who have been prey to depression will know just how this sense of impending doom feels.

would find its way inside of her. But no. There were two angels, shimmering with a light brighter inside the cave than the blazing sun outside. They asked her what was the matter, **their heavenly voices bouncing off the walls of this very earthly space**. And she told them, trying to hide the disappointment in her voice. If the very messengers of God didn't know where he was, what hope was there?

Blinking back tears, she could feel the birds circling closer now, their ragged black shapes blocking out the sun. Squinting to see past them, she saw another man, just another man. Those words again, 'What is the matter?' That's when she started babbling, a string of nonsense about going to find him and bringing him back to the grave. She could no more have borne to touch his battered corpse than she could have borne its weight to carry it back.

The birds swooped lower now, claws outstretched, beaks open, hungry for more of her. **'Mary', he said, and they were gone**. 'Mary' – her once shamed, then restored name. 'Mary.' Thank God.

She felt wounded at first by his words. Why? Why shouldn't she hold on to him, now she had found him again? Why shouldn't she grasp his hand, warm again now? Why shouldn't she **run her fingers down his face, clear and smooth again now**? But, as she turned away on an errand for him – she, Mary, charged with an errand by **this magnificent Jesus** – a strange thing happened. She never looked back. She never once checked over her shoulder to make sure he was still there. In the days and years that followed, she would never need to touch or see. He would ALWAYS be there. Instead of looking back, she looked up, smiled at the birds circling overhead, and felt only joy, not dread.

Mary, troubled by her demons flapping around her, needed to know that Jesus would always be there to keep them at bay. **Just like some of you** with old sins snapping at your heels like

their heavenly voices bouncing off the walls of this very earthly space – this is a rare moment where visitors from heaven are seen on earth. The image evokes its strangeness and wonder.

'Mary', he said, and they were gone – as with his command to the wind and the waves earlier in the Gospel, the response is instant.

run her fingers down his face, clear and smooth again now – the imagery here is so intense that it is almost sexual. However, we must recognise that the depths of Mary's rescue by Jesus are reflected in the intensity of her emotions.

this magnificent Jesus – strange and unnerving though this unexpected Jesus may be, there is a majesty to him.

Just like some of you – at this point, a third voice is introduced – a feature which we shall examine in Chapter 6.

dogs which have slipped the leash. Or bad memories swirling before your eyes, like thick smoke that makes you blink. EASTER means never having to look over your shoulder and check that he is there. Rather, it means knowing that he is. Calling for his help and knowing that the clap of his hands – or the word of his mouth – will send your demons running.

Positive aspects

There were not many comments passed on the day that this was preached, although the 'pregnant' silence immediately afterwards suggested a profound impact. The one comment which I remember came from a young woman whose life at the time was very complicated. Like Mary, she had both the demons of yesterday and the sadness of today with which to contend. It was her first visit to a morning service, and her only comment was 'Wow'.

Negative aspects

It is a calculated risk to choose an abstract image to dominate the narrative. Here, the image of the birds as Mary's thoughts and demons is vital to the sermon. That said, the direct identity between the two was never specified. This meant that some failed to grasp the sermon's central message of transformation, since they couldn't, in a sense, see Mary's problem.

Alternative approaches

This story certainly lends itself to a narrative approach, since it depicts such an intimate moment in the Easter story. It allows us to see the cataclysmic effects of the resurrection in microcosm as they affect Mary and her world. That said, it could have been tackled with more 'obvious' imagery or described by an invented observer hiding in the shadows of the garden.

Second-voice narrative: a summary

When it comes to the use of the second voice in narrative preaching, we are on familiar territory. We have been taught to recognise this voice from the earliest days of childhood. This is good, but it means that the preacher must strive just that little bit harder for arresting imagery. If he or she finds it, the second-voice narrative offers a vehicle of great power and beauty for God's truth.

Chapter 6

Preaching with the third voice

In the summer of 1982, I was privileged to travel around much of Germany with a school friend as we recovered from the exigencies of our exams. One Sunday morning, I found myself in Aachen cathedral. This magnificent building is a testament to the skill and faith of those who built it. Its clean simple lines, its soaring arches and beautiful ceilings – all speak of the glory of God. In the octagonal dome, there is a stone throne in the balcony – a seat for the Emperor Charlemagne himself. So great was the skill of the architects that the morning sun shines directly through the window opposite and illuminates the throne – on the Emperor's birthday each year. No visitor can be left in any doubt that this is truly a house of God.

However, on the Sunday in question, I was in no mood to appreciate this theological architecture. The service which was in progress was held largely in German (of which I understood some), with other elements in Latin (of which I understood none). I was trying to manage the linguistic acrobatics of comprehending what was going on, as well as the more physical feat of standing, sitting and kneeling at the right moments. Some may have been awed by the majesty of the building, and inspired by the musical excellence of the worship, but I was definitely not among them. As an Englishman with no experience of Roman Catholic worship in my own tongue, let alone another two, I was not in the mood to be inspired! In short, the worship did not suit me.

Despite all that we have said about the merits of using the narrative voice in preaching, we have to acknowledge that some will struggle to relate to it. Emotional first-voice narratives and beautifully crafted second-voice sermons may leave them as unmoved as the choir's songs and the architects' pillars left me on that bright summer morning in the cathedral. In any congregation, there will be analytical people and instinctive people; extroverts and introverts; right-brainers and left-brainers. In fact, just to make things even more complicated, the same people may find themselves differently inclined on different Sundays. This means that there will be occasions when people do not long for the breathless immediacy of the eye-witness account, nor the soft lilt of the storyteller's voice, but what they crave most of all is the voice of their pastor, their tried and trusted shepherd, pointing them in the direction of God's truth.

It is for this reason that we must add to the narrative repertoire the third-voice narrative. In this technique, either of the previous two styles can be combined with a more conventional explanation and application. This may precede the narrative, follow it as a conclusion, or be interwoven as an excursus in the middle of it. In this way, the narrative voice can be combined with other, more familiar voices as preacher and people chart their way into unexplored sermonic territory.

Benefits of using the third voice

Ensures application

One of the great advantages of the third-voice approach is that both preacher and people can be assured that application will take place. Instead of leaving the congregation to make up their own minds about how the sermon should be applied, the preacher does it for them. In much the same way as a more traditional approach, the preacher takes the lessons drawn out within the story and applies them to the lives of his or her hearers. For many, especially when they are unfamiliar with the narrative approach, this can be reassuring. It allows the preacher to use his or her hard-earned knowledge and understanding of the congregation to maximum effect. Within my own congregation, this has often proved to be the most popular approach. It allows the creative people to engage with the story and to learn from it, while the more analytical people can digest the application.

Lessens concentration on the medium

Another advantage of this approach is that it reduces the concentration on the actual medium of the sermon, directing it instead to its theological content. Despite everything we have said about the pursuit of creative excellence in preaching, we are not seeking to impress or entertain. If the thing which people remember most about a sermon is the brilliance of its storytelling or the evocative images that it used, we should regard this as a failure. Our aim is to make people different, rather than simply to give them a different experience. The use of a third voice directs people away from the seductive imagery and rhythm of the story and back to the urgent need for application of theological truths in their daily living.

Drawbacks of using the third voice

Overly narrow application

Conversely, one of the great drawbacks of this approach is that it *does* provide a precise application. Instead of leaving the congregation with a kind of productive ambiguity where they are bound to make their own application, it does the work for them. This inevitably means that some will 'dodge' the sermon's impact by deciding that they are not its intended target on this occasion. Whenever there is a precise application by the preacher, there is an equally precise application by the listener … to the lives of other people! As soon as the preacher commits to a particular application of a narrative, it thereby closes the door on others. While this happens to a certain extent with the choice of a narrator in the first voice, or the particular choice of vocabulary with the second, it is much more pronounced with third-voice narrative.

Destruction of narrative impact

Destruction is a very strong word to use. However, a clumsy application can have exactly the same effect as explaining a piece of music or analysing a poem. It brings a clash of left and right brain, of creative and analytical thought. A 'moment', carefully crafted through linguistic skill under the guidance of the Holy Spirit, can be lost in an instant if not carefully done. Furthermore, it runs the risk of turning the narrative into a simple illustration with no teeth.

Basic technique for using the third voice

As with the other techniques we have described, there are a number of issues which need to be considered at the outset. Clearly, the storytelling techniques themselves draw on those skills outlined in Chapters 4 and 5. Our issues here are connected with when and how to insert the 'third' voice of explanation, and what it should say when we do!

Pick your theme

The most fundamental question you need to ask yourself with a third-voice sermon is: what is it about? You should be able to state in a sentence or two what this sermon is for. While taking full account of the sovereignty of God and the gracious work of the Holy Spirit, what do you want it to achieve? Is it about grace or judgement? Is it set to challenge or to reassure? Clarity at this point will enable you to make the right decisions later on. You need to decide on this even *after* you have selected a Bible passage and title. We all know that the same passage can be preached numerous different ways by different preachers. Furthermore, even those preachers could preach their sermons based on the same passage and under the same theme and still come up with radically different emphases. Get on your knees and find out what the sermon is really about before you go any further. Ask God what he wants to say from *this* passage to *these* people on *this* occasion.

Pick your place

Having picked your theme and your passage, you now need to decide how you will position yourself in relation to the Biblical passage. In this third-voice preaching, you really have only one option. You cannot place yourself *behind* the passage, as you would in a first-voice narrative, simply allowing it to speak for itself. This leaves you unable to comment or apply. Equally, you cannot place yourself in front of the passage, making your application with only occasional references to the passage from which it was drawn, as some might in a more traditional propositional sermon. No, the only possible place from which you can preach is beside it, neither hiding behind the story nor standing in front of it to obscure it.

Pick your moment

Now that you have decided what the sermon is about, and where you will stand in relation to the story, you must pick your moment to intervene with the 'third' voice of explanation and application. There are a number of options to consider. You might choose to do this right at the outset, during the sermon's introduction. This is a style employed in Sermon 6.1 below, 'The pearl of great price'. This gives you the opportunity to introduce your theme and 'wake up' your listeners to the subtle ways in which you have woven it into the narrative. Alternatively, you can save it for the end. Having stimulated the senses and the imagination, you can then ensure that an application is made before the congregation goes home. This will particularly suit your analytical listeners. It can provide a useful apologetic for the narrative approach. The final alternative is to dip in and out of the third voice. This means that neither the narrative enthusiasts nor the narrative sceptics lose interest. This is the technique used in Sermon 6.3, 'The death of expectation'.

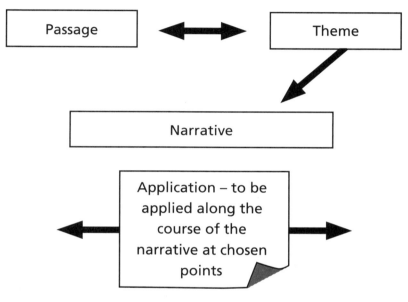

Figure 6.1: Preparing a third-voice sermon

Sermon 6.1
The pearl of great price
(Matthew 13:44–6)

Context

This sermon was preached at an evening service as part of a series on the Kingdom of God. Its aim was to heighten the listeners' awareness of their privilege at being part of the Kingdom.

Preparation

Theme

The fundamental theme here is our value in the eyes of God. This is explored in both the narrative and the expository elements of the sermon.

Place

The choice has been made to stand beside the passage from the outset – directing the listeners into it at the start, and helping them to climb back out of it at the end.

Moment

As you will see, there are two moments at which the switch is made from third voice to second and back again. There were two reasons for this. Firstly, it was to ensure that this important theme of self-worth and God-worth was anchored in the minds and hearts of the listeners. Secondly, it was preached at a time when the congregation was still relatively unaccustomed to a narrative style, and it therefore guided them through it.

The pearl of great price (Matthew 13:44–6)

A question for you – **how much is your human life worth?** How much is it actually worth? If we look at it in brutal chemical terms (someone did the calculations for me a few years ago, so this is probably out of date now and you are worth even less), it is a little bit under £100. If you bring it down to a little bit of potassium, a little bit of sodium, a little bit of calcium and so on, and you put all those things together, it's really not very much. Less than £100 if

Analysis of Sermon 6.1

how much is your human life worth? – here, in this first sentence, is a
statement of what the sermon is all about.

you look at it in brutal chemical terms. If you were to ask a 'human trafficker', if you were to ask someone waiting to load you into the back of his truck or van in the port of Calais, 'How much is human life worth?', he would quote you somewhere between £2,000 and £5,000 to take the risk and be brought across the Channel into this country. What is life really worth? Is it £100, is it £2,000–£5,000? Perhaps we should assess the value of human life on the basis of productivity? What can people produce? If they can produce a lot, they're worth a lot. If they can produce a little, they are worth a little. Well, that's all very well for the young and fit and healthy and strong, but where would it leave the old and the weak, if we were only worth what we can produce? Where does it leave all of us if we are only worth something if we are beautiful? How do you assess the value of human life? Is it just the bare necessities? Is it just what you know; is it just what you can do? Because if it is, then we live in an entirely brutal universe. But what if there were another way of assessing it? What if the value of our lives were not to be measured by what we do or what we have or by the way we look or by what we can produce? What if there were another way of telling what you and I were worth? Something else entirely? Why, that would change everything.

I want you to enter a different world with me. I want you to imagine a story with me. I don't know what you do when you listen to stories. Maybe you shut your eyes; maybe you kick off your shoes and stretch out? **You can do either of those things if you want to**. I want you now to enter this story with me. It's the story of two men. One of them is rich and the other one is poor.

Every day, the poor man goes about his business. **Day after day. Week after week.** It's not easy, life is hard, but by sheer graft, the sweat of his brow and the work of his hands, he just manages to scrape together enough to feed his family. It's a long hard day

You can do either of those things if you want to – on this particular occasion, the switch between third and second voice was made very obvious. For those new to the style, it reassured them about what was going on. However, it also ran the inherent risk of people not taking what followed seriously, since it was 'only a story'.

Day after day. Week after week – the use of rhythm is important in storytelling, and will be echoed again in the story of the rich man, in order to tie the two together.

every day. He leaves the house just as the inky blue of the night sky is turning pink. He comes back tired with his shoulders bowed just as the last rays of the sun are bouncing off the furrows. But he just manages to hold it together. And then fate turns on him. All of a sudden, the land refuses to yield to him any more. It shuts its mouth tight, like an **unwilling banker asked for a loan, or a tight-lipped and critical auntie asked for praise**. Like the drawstrings of a friend's purse snapping shut just when you needed them. And nothing will grow.

And as autumn follows summer and as winter follows autumn, he looks around at the pinched faces of his children. He looks with shame at the pitifully small amounts he is putting on their plates. And reluctantly he decides that the time has come to sell his land and to farm another man's land for him. He feels a great sense of shame and a feeling of sickness deep down in the pit of his stomach as he stands and he hands over the title deeds. He feels sure that just behind him he can feel his father, and just behind him, he can see the shadowy figure of his grandfather, and just behind him is his great-grandfather. And all of them are pointing a bony finger at him for selling out. Oh, the shame as he caves in, gives up and hands over the only thing the family ever had. But what can he do? His children are starving, his wife is desperate. And that's his only way out.

So another day dawns, early again. Just as night turns to day, he's out again and the gate slams shut behind him. But this time he doesn't walk to his own field. He turns and walks down the road, and, with a sigh, he harnesses the plough to the oxen and starts to push the plough before him. **Plodding up and down, up and down, turning another man's clods of earth on another man's farm with another man's plough with another man's oxen for another man's profit**. He feels like nothing, doing another man's

unwilling banker asked for a loan, or a tight-lipped and critical auntie asked for praise – deliberately anachronistic images, which sit in the now of the listener, rather than the then of the story.

Plodding up and down, up and down, turning another man's clods of earth on another man's farm with another man's plough with another man's oxen for another man's profit – the heaping up of these descriptions emphasises the hopelessness of the man's situation.

dirty work for him. Day follows day in the same dreary pattern, up and out and harnessing the oxen and ploughing the fields until suddenly there is a harsh **clink**, of metal on metal as the plough cuts through the earth. He bends down and rubs the earth from the metal with his callused fingers. Gold, glittering gold! Bending down and scrabbling in the fresh earth, he's breathless now, heart pounding. He can't believe what he sees. There's lots of it – coins, bangles and brooches, precious, beautiful things put away for safe keeping long ago. He squints up at the cloudless sky and he smiles. For once, things are going his way. **'Finders keepers!' he yells, because that's what the rabbis say**.

He bends down again, starts to shovel the earth back into the hole and to cover up his great discovery. He runs home from the field, not at the end of the day this time – the sun is still high in the sky. He lets the gate bang shut behind him. He begins to fly around the house, picking up anything of value: a piece of jewellery here, a plate there, something his mother gave him, hurling things together as his astonished family look on. In precisely one hour, he stands in his master's porch, heart in his mouth, and the money in his hand, handing it over and buying the plot of land.

Meanwhile, far away on the coast, with the sun glittering down on a sparkling ocean, **another man** goes about his business. There is no dirt and earth here, just sheer class. He walks around with no grime, no speck of dirt. The only noise that follows him is the swish of his garments, his long robes as he walks through the market place. Occasionally there is a **clink of metal** on metal as the rings on his chubby fingers knock together. This man has a fortune, a veritable fortune. This man has merchants ply their trade as far as the eye can see. At ports up and down the country, **the colours on the sails of his ships** are known by everyone. He is

clink – an audio 'clue' after so much visual imagery provides a good contrast.

'Finders keepers!' he yells, because that's what the rabbis say – the raising of the voice keeps some texture in the story and ensures a longer attention span by the listener. Also, this explains the authentic ruling of the day concerning buried treasure.

another man – despite his considerable wealth and influence, he is just 'another man'. This fits in with the sermon's overall theme about the value of human life.

clink of metal – an audio clue, to 'plug into' one of the five senses. Also a deliberate echo of the sound heard by the poor man in the field.

the colours on the sails of his ships – an authentic detail about rich merchants, revealed through research in Bible dictionaries.

a rich, rich man. His house is paved with cool marble – no heat of the day there – and its furnishings are draped with purple cloth. His table is graced every day with the finest meats and the richest spices. But he's not happy.

You see, one thing, just one thing, eludes him. And he wanders to and fro, like a little boy who's **lost his teddy**, trying to look for it. **Day after day**. And whenever he's in port on business, he just can't resist making his way down to the quayside where the boats are, because today, maybe just today, it will be there, and then everything will fall into place. He knows that the young men have been out at sea, he knows they have been out there pitching themselves off the boats, all but bursting their lungs to dive down into the depths to bring up those glittering pearls. And he wants to see what they have found.

He ignores the yells of the fishermen holding up their baskets and offering him the things they have caught. He ignores the beggars throwing themselves at his perfumed feet; he cuts a path straight to the quayside. **There's the boy. There he is. And the tables there and the baskets there.** And he sees the oysters scattered around on the flagstones. And it's there, today it's there. The most perfect pearl he's ever seen – fat and round and glistening and worth absolutely everything to him.

In a flash, fingers are clicked and servants are summoned and porters come running. All his goods are sold to willing buyers. And he walks home that day with no flowing robes, clutching the precious, faultless pearl in his now ringless hand. **He lifts it to his face, feels its icy smoothness on his cheek, smells the good ocean on it**. And he knows that he is content at last.

Do you know something? The amazing thing is that the man in both stories is the same. And it's not you and it's not me, and it's not all the other tens of thousands of Christians around the

lost his teddy – once again, an anachronistic detail to link the then and the now. Also, it emphasises that there is something truly pathetic about this rich and influential man.

Day after day – a deliberate echo of the poor man's story.

There's the boy. There he is. And the tables there and the baskets there – staccato phrases reflect the rich man's breathless excitement at this moment.

He lifts it to his face, feels its icy smoothness on his cheek, smells the good ocean on it – it is important to use this very tactile language here. For all his apparent sophistication, the rich man has feelings like the poor one.

Do you know something? – here, the switch back into the third voice is made obvious.

world. The person in both stories is God himself. *Just like it is in the story of the weeds and the tares being sown together.* **Just like it is afterwards in the story of God casting his net and catching the fish**. The man in both stories is God himself, who, like the poor man, would sell everything just to have you. God who, like the rich man, has everything at his beck and call – the skies and the seas and the galaxies that you and I have never even dreamt of – and yet all of it is not enough to make him happy until he has you. That's how much your life is worth.

Last week, I visited a memorial in a place called Thiepval, in the middle of the Somme battlefield. It towers over the countryside, visible for mile after mile after mile. And when you go and you stand inside, all these apparently smooth stones are not smooth at all. Every square inch is covered with names – Herberts and Franks and Arthurs – 72,000 of those who are not buried elsewhere. You stand there in the shadow; you stand inside, literally surrounded by those names – and something, a little something of the cost starts to come home to you.

I want to ask you to stand for a moment now. Just stand – and, as you close your eyes, recognise how much you are worth. Stand there and let it sink in that God would give his most precious thing to have you. That God as the creator of the universe, of the rolling oceans and the stars and the planets, could never be content until he brought you home.

Positive aspects

This richly descriptive narrative certainly held the attention of the congregation, both in my own church and when it was preached to an audience of pastors in India. Furthermore, the unexpected interpretation of God as the subject of the parable of finding the treasure gave many pause for thought.

Just like it is in the story of the weeds and the tares being sown together. Just like it is afterwards in the story of God casting his net and catching the fish – since the sermon propounds a slightly unorthodox interpretation of this story, it is important to demonstrate where it was derived from.

Last week, I visited – a further step away from the story and into the 'real' world.

I want to ask you to stand – the physical act of standing prevents the sermon from being a purely cerebral experience. For kinetic learners, this will help to reinforce what they have heard.

Negative aspects

Ironically, it is exactly this same point which caused problems for many listeners. They found themselves so caught up with this unexpected interpretation of the parables that they spent the rest of the service puzzling over its veracity, rather than savouring its truth about their worth to God.

Alternative approaches

It could have worked well to preach this still with a narrative approach, but to concentrate instead on just one of the two parables. In this way, the point could have been made in a simple, direct way. Equally, the allusion to the Thiepval monument could have been omitted, since this introduced another narrative element to an already busy sermon.

Sermon 6.2
Leaving the comfort zone
(Luke 8:26–39)

Context

This sermon was preached as part of a series on growing up as a Christian. During the series, the different steps of growing up, such as birth, learning to walk, learning to talk and so on, were all mirrored with similar stages in our maturing as Christians. This sermon, which mirrored the stage where children start to leave the parental home, was preached about two thirds of the way through the series. It was also preached at a 150th church anniversary service, with an emphasis on the need to look not back but forward.

Preparation

Theme

The theme here, as reflected in the title, is all to do with moving on in the Christian life. There is also an element of moving people on from initial naïve interpretations of this passage and confronting them with its more uncomfortable elements, such as the destruction of the pigs and the refusal by Jesus to let the man accompany him.

Place

For the most part, the preacher stands in relation to the narrative as a storyteller here, throwing light onto the story and allowing its vivid colours to live. The preacher also acts as a bridge, inserting words and phrases which link the then of the story with the now of the listener.

Moment

The decision was made to bring in the third voice only after the story, so as to let its power speak for itself. Thus, the third voice comes in to apply the lessons learnt only after the listeners have been left with a profound impression of the dramatic events in the story. In this way, the application finds a more susceptible home than it might have done if it were brought up in advance.

Leaving the comfort zone (Luke 8:26–39)

As the boat nosed into the reeds at the water's edge with a gentle **swish**, Jesus and the others climbed out, their feet splashing in the water and the shingle **crunching** underfoot. At once the air was shattered with a tortured, animal cry. The wild man stumbled out from among the tombs, broken chains swaying from side to side, their sharp edges **slapping** on his raw, wounded sides. His eyes were bloodshot, his body caked with his own filth; **the stench** was appalling.

'What do you want with me, Jesus?' he slurred. His voice was distorted and ugly, a man shouting into a chamber of his own echoes. Jesus' voice was calm, interested. Looking at the **twisted, broken man** at his feet, he asked him his name. **It was a long time since anyone had asked him that**. So long, in fact, that the voices within shouted him down and came tumbling out of his mouth like a horde of banshees. 'Legion', they said and began to plead for themselves. Jesus' reply, when it came, was in an altogether different voice. He spoke like an ageless God. Wrapping his words around the situation, like God framing the heavens and the earth. One word from him, and **all hell broke loose**.

It started with a restlessness in the herd of pigs, up beyond the gravestones. They began to grunt and squeal, churning up the ground and sending up clouds of dust in their agitation. Then it came. **Like things possessed**, they thundered down the hill to its edge over the water. As if pursued by some invisible hunter, they threw themselves into the water below. One, two, hundreds, all driven on by some madness. The water itself seemed to **boil and foam** as they thrashed and kicked and sank out of sight.

Then all was quiet – and, as the waters settled back, so the wild man himself seemed to deflate. The anger and agitation were

Analysis of Sermon 6.2

swish ... crunching ... slapping – onomatopoeic words in order to 'capture' the listener. Furthermore, the word 'slapping' evokes some of the pain which the man must have felt.

the stench – a deliberately provocative word.

twisted, broken man – it is important to acknowledge that the whole person is broken, and not just the mind.

It was a long time since anyone had asked him that – the narrative style allows us to put flesh on the bones of a Bible character and to 'fill in' their story. There is a serious point here too. The man's condition had meant that people treated him as less than human, never stopping to ask his name.

all hell broke loose – the use of this phrase crosses the bridge between then and now. While it is theologically true that 'hell is breaking loose' at this point, it is also a phrase in common parlance which brings some welcome familiarity in a strange tale of demon possession and pigs!

Like things possessed – again, a proverbial expression. Of course they are not like things possessed, they *are* things possessed; but the phrase is familiar and helpful at this point.

boil and foam – in contrast to the bucolic scene with which we started, and to which we shall return shortly, this is an image of real and disturbing violence in the natural world – as indeed the episode would have been.

gone. From somewhere in the crowd, a simple robe appeared, and he slipped it on like a man who had never forgotten how to dress. Smoothing it over his generous muscles, he sat and gazed up at Jesus, drinking in the very sight of his face. He looked up at him, like a man looking at the surgeon who has saved his life, and a delicious peace descended on the lake again. **Birds sang, water lapped at the shore once more**.

Soon, it was shattered as a crowd appeared from all around. Some were familiar – the local strong-arms who had put the wild man in chains … and their wives who'd hidden their children as they had done so. Others were farmers and fishermen. Some were even religious, in their own way. Eyes darted from one to the other, hoping for a spokesman. 'Go', the spokesman said at last. 'Go away, and take your power with you.' For all his bluster, he was frightened and the whole town with him. 'Just go, please, Jesus of Nazareth. Just leave us be.'

Harsh words **for the healer, but harsher still were the words from the healer**. As he climbed back into the boat, and his new friend strode to climb in with him, he held up a hand. 'No', he said just as firmly as before. 'You must stay. Go back to the people who know you. **Tell them your story, show them your sanity**. Don't come, you must stay here for me.' Cruel words, and so hard to fulfil. As the boat faded on the horizon, the man picked his way through the crowd, all of them stepping aside to let him through. Ahead lay all kinds of explanations, all manner of questions, and an uncertain welcome wherever he went.

Why did Jesus say it? **Why** not give the man a break? Let him come in the boat. **Would it** really have hurt? In fact, he says this kind of thing often enough. He says it in Mark's version of the story too. He says it to the weeping Mary in John chapter 20 verse 17. He says it to the disciples as they watch him ascend into heaven:

Birds sang, water lapped at the shore once more – a conscious return to peaceful imagery by way of contrast.

Soon, it was shattered – the narrative style often demands that we 'telescope' events which may actually have been some time apart. This maintains the pace of the storytelling.

for the healer, but harsher still were the words from the healer – not the kind of thing the congregation are expecting to hear about Jesus, but it alerts them to Jesus' apparently severe rebuke which follows.

Tell them your story, show them your sanity – a deliberate use of the word 'story'.

Why ... Why ... Would it – the 'piling up' of these questions gives voice to the puzzlement that many will feel at Jesus' apparently harsh words.

Stale Bread?

'Go, reach the world for me'. **He says it sometimes to us**. 'Don't stay in this church ... this job ... this place. Don't stay here on safe ground. Don't leave things as they have always been.'

Why? Because we're entrusted with the expansion of an unbuilt kingdom and we must move on, like Jesus, relentlessly pushing himself on to crowd after crowd. Do you know what that man reminds me of as he watches the boat disappear until it is a tiny dot on the horizon? He reminds me of Christians gazing wistfully back at some sermon that moved them or some service that blessed them *years ago*, and they keep on playing the tape of it until it is almost worn out. That is not the point! **The Jews died if they ate yesterday's manna – God's good provision turned bad inside them**. We cannot survive on a diet of yesterday's blessings and expect still to complete the journey. There are many, many parallels between the development of a child and the development of the Christian. As the child learns to talk, so we learn to pray. As the child learns to walk by taking risks and moving from one safe piece of furniture to another, so we learn to move from one haven to another, trusting in the goodness of God. If a child is still living at home thirty or forty years after they were born, we think it odd. And yet plenty of Christians are still living in the playpen. If they have got out of the cot, that is!

Jesus has rescued us and saved us. Certainly because he loves us, but also because he loves THEM ... and needs our gifts to reach them. The New Testament is stuffed with images of growing ... growing up. To linger where we are spiritually is to choose stunted growth, and to choose stunted growth is to deprive the world. If the man had gone with Jesus, stayed in that comfy boat, how many people would not have heard?

It must have been a long walk home for the man. It must have been a test even to remember where home was! There must have

He says it sometimes to us – this is the point at which we cross back into the third voice. 'It' could stand here for any number of specific demands which God has made of the listeners.

The Jews died if they ate yesterday's manna – God's good provision turned bad inside them – with its concentration on the 'little stories', it is important that narrative preaching does not lose sight of the overall sweep of Biblical history.

It must have been – here, we almost switch back to the narrative voice as we picture the man making the long journey home.

been many awkward conversations. BUT he did it. By doing so, he sowed the seed for all the mission (in Acts) which was to come. Don't stay still – move on!

Positive aspects

The strong narrative element of this story meant that people were already engaged by the time the more specific life-application was given. Since it touches on a raw theme of our fears about moving on, many were able to identify with it. The use of the third voice enabled them to see that this powerful story sits within the context not only of the Gospel but of their own lives too.

Negative aspects

Some were so caught up in the depiction of the story that they found it hard to make the switch to the contemporary application. They might have found it easier either to have the whole thing in a narrative style, or the whole thing in a more devotional style. This is a risk in combining the two approaches.

Alternative approaches

This sermon would have lent itself well to a first-voice narrative. That voice could have either been the voice of the man in the story himself, or that of a supplementary character in the crowd or on the lakeside. Equally, it can be preached in a more conventional way by drawing out the lessons concerning our attachment to destructive lifestyles and our obsession with holding onto special moments.

Sermon 6.3
The death of expectation
(John 5:1–11)

Context

This sermon was preached as part of a series on John's Gospel, to a large congregation, most of whom were familiar with the story. Typically, it would include those nursing disappointments of various kinds, and those who envy the spiritual experiences and blessings of others – as would many congregations!

Preparation

Theme

The key theme here is one of faith and disappointment. It demonstrates how accumulated disappointment can not only sap our ability to hope but also eclipse our inclination to believe.

Place

The narrator stands beside the story here – maybe lingering just out of sight in the portico so that he can see both the man talking to Jesus and the little beetle on the floor behind him.

Moment

The third voice is brought in at two moments here. The first is at the outset, in order to introduce us to the principal character and to highlight the theme. This signals to the listeners that the very specific story which follows nonetheless articulates a general theme. The second intervention of the third voice comes between Jesus' offer of healing and the man's reply. In this way, we are encouraged to straddle two worlds – the story's and our own.

The death of expectation (John 5:1–11)

The death of expectation can be the slowest death of all. One minute, the candle is burning proud and tall at the head of its wax column ... the next it is sputtering and dying in a pool of discarded wax. And all the time the light is fading – but so slowly that no-one notices.

It had been like that for him – his expectations lowered **day after day**. At first, like all the other hopefuls, he had expected to dash into the water when the angel came. He didn't know how he would do it, not with these useless legs **God had cursed him with** – but he would have done somehow. Crawling, perhaps, or rolling like a barrel, scattering people as he went – it wouldn't have mattered. In his dream, the people all clapped and cheered as he passed by. But their cheers were just a fantasy – and, as day followed day, that expectation withered and died, like his legs.

After that, it was the expectation that he might see the water when the angel stirred it. At the very least, he might watch as others were healed. But thirty-eight years is a long time. Younger men had come since then, men with families and friends to carry them when the moment came. By now, even his view of the water was obscured. Way back, underneath the colonnade, his day was spent looking at **the twisted backs and the passing healthy feet of others**.

As expectation died, and hopes withered, tiny things became absorbing. Today, he was watching a beetle in the dust by his

Analysis of Sermon 6.3

The death of expectation can be the slowest death of all – here, we make it very obvious what the sermon's theme will be. The use of the general in the third voice leads us into the particular in the second.

day after day – rhythm is important in this narrative, in order to capture the relentless monotony of the man's existence.

God had cursed him with – not only an expression of how the man felt, but also of the theology of his day whereby sickness was deemed to be the curse of God.

After that – this tracks the gradual diminution of his hope.

the twisted backs and the passing healthy feet of others – in good narrative, as in skilful film-making, different points of view can help to keep things interesting.

wretched feet. For hours on end, it had been struggling to roll a morsel of bread away from the crowd – to feed its young, perhaps. The morsel was two or three times its size, and many times it had rolled back on top of the hapless creature, mocking its efforts. **'Give up,' the man mouthed – 'it's easier in the end.'** But the creature would not give up, and was rallying from its last defeat, when the man's view was obscured.

Two sandalled feet stood in his way. 'Do you want to get well?' asked a voice above him. He allowed his gaze to travel up from the feet, the legs, the body, to the face which looked down at him. 'WANT to get well?' – what kind of a question was that?

There was no point wanting – **want fuelled desire, and desire fed off his disappointment, and then he was eaten away inside, as he had been outside**. And so he explained the whole sorry tale. He told how he had come here year after year. He told how he had struggled alone to get into the water when the moment came. He explained how he had watched time after time as others splashed and danced in the healing waters.

'No,' he finished, 'I cannot.' **And his eyes dropped to the ground again as the beetle scurried away, leaving its prize behind.**

If we had been there, enjoying shade from the sun under the portico. If we had overheard the conversation between Jesus and this helpless, hopeless man. What would we have said? Would we have *stood* before him and said 'don't you want to get well?' Or would we have *sat* with him and said 'don't get your hopes up?' They are unfair questions, since we have all read the story and know how it ends.

BUT we also know how it is repeated – day after day, week after week in many homes and lives … many of them here. Ongoing need and crisis seems to sap us of our capacity to hope, like a tiny bulb in the car, secretly sapping the battery until one day the

'Give up,' the man mouthed – 'it's easier in the end' – the device of the beetle gives the man scope to express some of his deepest feelings.

Two sandalled feet stood in his way – once again, a novel point of view is introduced. Disabled listeners will appreciate that their physical perspective on the world is different to that of those who can stand erect.

want fuelled desire, and desire fed off his disappointment, and then he was eaten away inside, as he had been outside – this relentless logic expresses his feeling of being trapped.

And his eyes dropped to the ground again as the beetle scurried away, leaving its prize behind – the beetle's action imitates the man's inner decision as he all but refuses Jesus' help.

If we had been there – at this point, we cross back into the third voice. In this sermon, it is done in a particularly obvious way, so as to confront the listeners with this specific question – what would you have done?

engine won't start. We don't mean to get that way. We don't even notice. BUT – before we know where we are, we think that our problem is insurmountable and we just have to live with it.

'Get up', said the voice. It wasn't harsh … but it wasn't soft either. It was an old voice – older than the stone walls around him, older even than the earth on which he lay. 'Get up, and take that mat with you.' Like a child trying out his legs for the first time, gingerly he levered himself up, the familiar dust grinding into his palms as he pushed down. He was level with the man who had spoken now. He could look into the face of this – this saviour. Was it his imagination – or could he hear the applause he had dreamt of so many times? Shaking his head, he looked down at his feet as if he had never seen them before. They looked different from up here.

As he bent down to roll up his mat, he noticed a beetle lumbering towards a hole in the wall with a morsel of bread on its back. With a gentle nudge of his finger, he helped it on its way. As he straightened, the stranger had gone, and he set off to explore the world from this new point of view.

Don't let disappointment sap your hope – God's voice is as old as the hills and as new as the sunrise, and it still has the power to change the unchangeable.

Positive aspects

The use of tiny details such as the beetle really made people think about this story. Instead of seeing the disabled man as some kind of stooge, there to feed Jesus' lines to him, they saw that he was a real person. Not only that, but also he was a real person nursing the same kind of hopes, disappointments and doubt in his heart that they do.

'Get up', said the voice – crossing back into the narrative, we hear the voice of Jesus once again.

trying out his legs for the first time – in crafting a narrative, it is important always to get behind the actions to the way they may have felt to the person performing them.

They looked different from up here – again, the use of different points of view or perspectives is important in this story.

With a gentle nudge of his finger, he helped it on its way – the man's treatment of the beetle mirrors Christ's treatment of him.

Don't let disappointment sap your hope – in closing, the third voice brings us back to the key subject matter as stated in the introduction.

Negative aspects

Some found the use of incidental details distracting, and were inclined to search for them in the text. For them, these elements of the imagination were a distraction from the central theme rather than an embellishment of it. Others may have found that the third-voice applications were in fact too narrow, and prevented them from 'inserting' their own particular experiences into the story.

Alternative approaches

Many of the same lessons could have been drawn out using a second-voice narrative. An observer in the portico, watching and listening to the exchanges between the man and Jesus, could have emphasised many of the same points without the need to jump between different voices.

Sermon 6.4
Ruth – friend for life (Ruth 1)

Context

This was initially preached as part of a series on different servants of God. It was then preached again at the chapel service in a Bible college. A number of those in the congregation on that occasion had burnt many boats and given up many things to be there – but were now facing serious questions about where such steps of faith might take them next.

Preparation

Theme

The key theme here is loyalty. This is explored obliquely through Ruth's ability to demonstrate it, and principally through Orpah's failure to do so. Ruth 1:16–17 contains such a well-known statement of loyalty that its aim was to draw attention to the theme elsewhere in the story.

Place

It is precisely because the story is so well known that the narrator stands right in the thick of the action, describing the actions 'up close and personal' in great detail. This ensures maximum impact before the application is made.

Moment

The power of this sermon lies in the story itself – the story of three women who began a journey, and two who completed it. In order to allow the story to have its maximum impact, all application is left to the end.

Ruth – friend for life (Ruth 1)

The packing didn't take long. They had lived simply these past ten years. There was a dull earthenware pot, which she wrapped carefully in a shawl. There was a bangle she had received on her wedding day. Feeling its **cool** metal against her skin, she had remembered the **warmth** of his **rough** hands as he had slipped it on. After that, there was a lock of his hair, a spare shawl and a little food for the journey. Then she stepped out into the sunshine and fell in with the others. At first the journey was pleasant, like so many of the walks they had taken together these past months since being on their own. There was a slight breeze on their faces, and it made the barley stalks hiss in the fields as they passed. **Pots clattered and dogs barked as their neighbours went about their business**. Some stopped as they swept the dust from the doorway of their houses, others hailed them from the fields, and some called them to stop and eat. The smell of cooking fires made them want to stop, but there was a long way to go.

By midday, with the sun beating down on them, **all the familiar faces were left behind**. No houses now, no waves and no more greetings from neighbours. Ahead of them lay Judah, a strange and distant place. At lunch, as they rested beneath a cypress tree, Naomi had urged them to go back. 'Go on,' she said. 'There's nothing for you **over there**. Go back to your mothers, and may they find husbands for you.' Naomi had choked on these last words, and the two of them comforted her as they had done so often lately. 'No,' they replied. 'We're coming with you' – and, with that, they picked up their burdens and continued the journey.

By late afternoon, all were tired, their pace slowing as the hours passed. The sun would set soon, and Judah would be nearer still. That's when Naomi had tried again. 'It's no good. God

Analysis of Sermon 6.4

The packing didn't take long – we go straight into the story with a very 'domestic' image. This is to be a story of ordinary people.

cool ... warmth ... rough – it is important to engage the senses early on in the story.

Pots clattered and dogs barked as their neighbours went about their business – since the sermon will deal with the lure of staying behind when God calls us on, this warm and appealing description of what they leave behind is important.

all the familiar faces were left behind – here, the same theme is stated in a more obvious way.

over there – a familiar shorthand for the strange place, be it over the road or over the sea, where we do not naturally fit in.

himself has cursed me, and you must leave me be. **I am bitter and disappointed**, but there's time for you yet. Now go!' And so the parting had come. Naomi's hug, like her faith, was weakened by her disappointment. Her tears were **warm** though, **wet** on the shoulders of her daughters-in-law as she cried them, and **chill** in the night air as they dried on the journey.

But now, now the journey is over. Every last weary step completed. The dust of the road seems to cling, **clogging every pore, coating every hair, clinging** like an unwelcome memory. The woman sets her possessions out again – the pot, the shawl, the precious lock of hair. There's something in her eyes as she looks towards the hills through the window. Is it regret ... or loneliness ... or hope for the future? *He* always used to say that her eyes hid more than they showed. Wiping a tear from them now, she shakes her head, turns her back on the **distant hills of Judah** and sweeps the earthen floor of her empty home. **Orpah** is here to stay.

Orpah's sister-in-law (who gives her name to this book) took a huge risk – going to an unfamiliar land where her accent stood out a mile and her only excuse for being there was a husband who was dead and gone. Loyalty and loyalty alone carried her over the border and into Bethlehem to face dear knows what (verse 22, 'Ruth the Moabitess'). That kind of open-ended, blind loyalty always carries a risk of rejection, feeling out of place, of tackling the unfamiliar. But it is just the kind of loving loyalty that God expects from us. Yes, he expects clear loyalty even when the destination is unclear – as he did with Moses, as he did with Abraham, and as he did with all the disciples called by Jesus.

To be a true servant of God means always being prepared to move on. Mentally, it means leaving old loyalties and prejudices and security blankets behind. Physically, it means leaving old

I am bitter and disappointed – the narrative style still allows you to explain things like the meaning of Naomi's name, but it is woven into the narrative.

warm … wet … chill – these sensual images underline the intimacy of their relationship and the real heartache of severing it.

clogging every pore, coating every hair, clinging – negative words, which echo the negative feelings which many harbour about making a journey away from the familiar for God's sake.

distant hills of Judah – the first hint that it is Orpah we are thinking about and not Ruth.

Orpah is here to stay – after the hint above, this is the real moment of revelation about the focus of our interest.

Orpah's sister-in-law (who gives her name to this book) took a huge risk – in the third voice, we can return to the Bible story in some detail.

To be a true servant of God – here, the real subject of the sermon is stated outright.

jobs, places, even countries behind (verse 16). To be a truly great Christian in God's eyes, you must be prepared to do just that. We must be prepared to *risk* everything in order to gain his approval, which *means* everything. The blessings of doing it are enormous. He not only promises you a destination but also gives his companionship on the way. But whenever God moves us on, there are always those who back away, who choose not to go on the journey, like the returnees from exile, for example. In their story, some seized the day and returned to the promised land, but others chose to stay where they were. We can see this in **John 6:66**, with Jesus himself too.

The story at the start is pure invention; we have no idea what actually happened to Orpah. We only know that she never made the journey. She never arrived in Bethlehem like the others. She never saw the family's joy when God reversed their misfortunes. She never became an ancestor of Jesus, as Ruth did.

If God is looking for your clear loyalty, will you give it? Or are you so set on having a clear destination that you're not prepared to follow him? If God is calling you to go somewhere, do something. **Don't be like Orpah and end up where you always were, filled with regrets**.

Positive aspects

Reactions to this sermon were extremely positive. When it was preached in the church, it helped to confirm a missionary call to a young couple which resulted in them leaving home, job and country. Later, they wrote as follows: 'when you preached this sermon, a heart-wrenching conviction, which I can only attribute to the Holy Spirit, grabbed me and wouldn't let me go. The staff of the good shepherd had struck me and it smarted. Recognition

John 6:66 – for those unfamiliar with the narrative style, direct textual allusions in the third voice can be reassuring.

The story at the start is pure invention – a direct allusion to the storytelling like this is unusual. However, in this instance it emphasises the difference between the invented story of Orpah and the real stories in the listeners' lives of missed opportunities.

Don't be like Orpah and end up where you always were, filled with regrets – at the end of the sermon, its purpose is restated in the third voice, so that no-one can be left in any doubt.

of who God is; obedience; love and loyalty matter in the story of Ruth. We didn't want to end up like Orpah – a nobody with no contribution to God's kingdom.' At the Bible college, it provoked an interesting description of 'using the ears as eyes'.

Negative aspects

The power of the story here is so absorbing that it is a real struggle to tear oneself away from it and listen to the application. Some were still left in Orpah's little house, staring out of the window, as the application drew to its close. Others would have found a clear statement of the theme at the outset, as we have seen in other third-voice sermons, more helpful.

Alternative approaches

This could have been preached powerfully as a first-voice narrative. We could have heard from Naomi, comparing the reactions of her two daughters-in-law. We could have heard from Orpah herself, or even from a supplementary character of a neighbour – watching her leave and then watching her return. While the themes of loyalty and fear could be brought out in a traditional propositional way, the richness of the story cries out for a narrative approach of some description.

Sermon 6.5
The wind of God (Acts 2:1–13)

Context

This sermon was preached at a service of Pentecost praise.
The service was a formal one, with a choir and band providing
music. In previous years, the sermon at this service had been a
more straightforward analysis of the theological implications of
Pentecost.

Preparation

Theme

The focus here is on the disturbing influence of the Spirit of God.
Through evocative images and provocative phrases, it seeks to
challenge the listeners about their relationship with the mighty
and unpredictable Spirit of God. It also sets the work of the Spirit
within the historical context of the whole of scripture.

Place

The narrator stands at some distance from the story, thereby
allowing him to take a long view and look back to creation and
forward to the Church. It is a short step from that position to the
very direct application which concludes the sermon.

Moment

The third voice is reserved until the end here, so as to allow the
atmosphere and images of the story itself to have the maximum
impact. The story needs no introduction, since it is very familiar

ground. Also, at a formal Pentecost service, everyone is expecting this passage to be preached, so it is better to get straight into the vivid narrative in order to preserve some freshness in the preaching.

The wind of God (Acts 2:1–13)

The wind had been a long time coming … **a long time coming**. Before there was man or beast, before time itself had been chopped into hours and minutes, **it played across the soupy surface of the planet as it slurped and bubbled**. At God's command, it had warmed the lifeless bodies of doll Adam and doll Eve, and they had walked and skipped in the garden of Eden.

Later, when the gates of the garden had slammed shut, it had found its way out into the world. It had blown sand in the face of God's enemies, whipped up the waves and washed them away. It had breathed on the sparks of God's mercy and made a fire from floor to ceiling to light them on their way. Later still, it had **blown dust from the scrolls of God's law in a temple storeroom**. It had tugged at the robes of a prophet here … ruffled his beard there. **Once it had bucked and dived through the valley of bones** – in and out of the carcasses, bringing life wherever it went. And the glory of God had ridden on its back into the temple, like a conquering hero on his mount.

On the darkest day it had held back, along with the sun and the angels as God's terrible mercy was etched on the tree. Now, down there, in among the thousands milling to and fro, there were some waiting for it to return. 'Wait in Jerusalem', the Lord had said – and, in obedient puzzlement, that's what they had done. Through tears, disappointment, even terror, they had

Analysis of Sermon 6.5

a long time coming – the repetition of this phrase gives it a very narrative 'feel' as the story begins.

it played across the soupy surface of the planet as it slurped and bubbled – here, a familiar phrase about the Spirit of God moving over the waters is given fresh life as visual images are used to describe it.

blown dust from the scrolls of God's law in a temple storeroom – in fact, this is an allusion to Hezekiah's reforms, sparked by the discovery of scrolls of the law during temple repairs. Listeners familiar with scripture will pick up on allusions like this, while for others they simply work as 'part of the story'.

Once it had bucked and dived through the valley of bones – similarly, those who know their Old Testament well will recognise an allusion here to Ezekiel's vision of the valley of the dry bones.

waited, like faithful sentinels told not to leave their posts. And now, at last, it came.

In through every window and funnelled down every alley it came. **It rattled and whistled and ruffled wherever it went.** A **curtain** was torn from its mounting here. A **jar** toppled from its table in the street there – shattering in a hundred unnoticed pieces. A barking **dog** flattened its ears and whined at this strange phenomenon. A child stuck out his pudgy arm to feel it, only to be snatched back by his protective mother. The robes of the priests **flapped round the grey heads of their wearers** and wrapped them up like clowns in a show. Many cowered, shielding eyes and faces from the dust. Jerusalem had never been like this before.

Only a few turned their faces up and smiled. Their time had come, their master's promise fulfilled. What they could see, as others looked away, was tongues of fire, borne on the wind. **They bucked and wriggled, danced and twisted like living things.** And to each faithful watcher – a flame came. As they stood closer together now, their faces took on the glow of each other's flame. The pallor of grief and worry was gone, a golden warmth in its place. What had looked like a wake a few minutes before now seemed like a birthday party. Theirs were **the faces of excited children, gathered round the candles on the cake for the big moment**, ready to sing with glad and simple hearts. Theirs were the faces of a church made new. Outside the room, the glow of the flames was like a campfire to the onlookers – **a beacon for the lost, a warning for the predator**. Borne on the wind, warmed by the flame, the Church was on the move.

And the church **still is** on the move. When it embraces the wind. When it throws open the windows and props open the doors. When it looks to God with **upturned faces**. THEN the flame of heaven burns within – a beacon for the lost and a warning for

It rattled and whistled and ruffled wherever it went – since part of the sermon's aim was to rescue Pentecost from the realm of the theoretical/mystical, very physical images are used here.

curtain ... jar ... dog – as we have seen before, small details can capture the big event very successfully. This is a technique employed to great effect by film-makers and radio correspondents.

flapped round the grey heads of their wearers – this was preached at the end of the week during which Pope John Paul II's funeral had taken place. During it, many had commented on how amusing the cardinals looked when the wind caught their scarlet robes and wrapped them around their heads.

They bucked and wriggled, danced and twisted like living things – again, a physical description for a familiar theological reality.

the faces of excited children, gathered round the candles on the cake for the big moment – when each individual flame was brought close together, the effect would be not unlike that of candlelight reflected on children's faces as they lean in together to blow out the candles on a birthday cake. Also, of course, Pentecost is the church's birthday.

a beacon for the lost, a warning for the predator – this phrase will be repeated more than once. It reflects the mixed blessing of the powerful Holy Spirit – a comforter to those on the inside, and a direct challenge to those on the outside.

still is – with these two words, we cross back into the third voice.

upturned faces – as often in narrative, a shorthand phrase is used – here, it summarises an attitude of trust in God.

the predator. When it shuts the windows and seals itself off. When it goes undisturbed about its terribly important business within. Then the wind sweeps on elsewhere, the fire dies in the hearth, and the sound of the celebration is lost forever.

In the middle of the twelfth century, the then Pope received a visit from a theologian as he was counting some of the Church's great riches. 'See,' he said, 'no longer can the Church say "silver and gold have I none".' 'That is true, Your Holiness,' the theologian replied, 'but nor can it say "rise up and walk".'

Today, the wind and flame of God have come again, and we keep them out at our peril.

Positive aspects

As soon as the service was over, one person commented to me that the sermon had made them realise how exciting Pentecost was. For that individual, the use of vivid and provocative images had bypassed the head and gone straight to the heart. For those who prefer a more cerebral approach, the use of the third voice at the end had reassured them that a serious theological point was being made about our response to the Spirit.

Negative aspects

To preach such a radically different sermon at such a high-profile event is a calculated risk. Some in the congregation deemed it inappropriate and felt that an opportunity to explain the meaning of Pentecost in plain terms with guests present had been lost.

Alternative approaches

The same narrative element could have been used, but with a third-voice introduction as well as a third-voice conclusion. This

Today – we finish the sermon clearly in the third voice.

may have reassured some about the serious intent of the sermon. It would also have made it possible to outline its thematic intent from the very beginning. The disadvantage of this is the curse of predictability: if we know where the sermon is going to end, why follow it there?

Third-voice narrative: a summary

For those who are new to narrative preaching, either as a preacher or as a listener, the third voice gives a helpful 'way in' to this new experience. It combines the surprise of the new with the comfort of the old, and engages different people in different ways. It allows for the creativity of the storyteller alongside the skills of the expositor. Clearly, there is a lot to commend this particular approach. However, there are times when the preacher should have the courage of his or her convictions, and allow the carefully crafted story to speak for itself. Like the other two voices, the third voice has its place in narrative preaching, but it should never be the only one we use.

Chapter 7

Encouraging the storyteller within

All over the world, in all different cultures, the storyteller is a very powerful figure. As Alistair Macintyre puts it in Jonathan Freedland's book *Jacob's Gift*, 'Man is a storytelling animal'.[6] As Christians, we would recognise that part of the *imago dei* within us is the ability and desire to tell stories, as he has done. In Native American culture, the Hopi Indians have a traditional figure of the storyteller in which a central figure is surrounded by the rapt faces of smaller people listening intently. Storytellers in many cultures are the guardians of heritage, the conduits of wisdom and the glue which holds the historical and cultural continuum together. All of this has now spilt over into more surprising areas too. Corporate America woke up to the power of storytelling in creating motivation and identity in the early 1990s, and it has since become a powerful tool in many companies in the UK too. A review of literature from executive coaching and personnel training will soon reveal that change-managers in industry and commerce are keen to harness the power of storytelling.

If the things you have read so far make you feel that storytelling is a weapon you should have in your preaching armoury, then it is time to start perfecting the techniques necessary to use it. As with any new skill, be it riding a bike or learning to paint, the initial steps are always the hardest. There is an uncomfortable naïvety which we all feel when entering new territory. How come everyone else seems to know what they are doing? The fact is that they don't – it's just that they have had more time to disguise their ignorance!

Preparing the storyteller

How long does it take you to write a sermon? I was once interviewed by the local newspaper about a nativity play I had produced that was acted entirely by adults. When asked how long it had taken to prepare, I replied: 'about ten years'. It had taken all that time for the idea to take shape within my mind, and to ready myself to write it and produce it. The longer we go on preaching, the more we realise that our times of preparation are as much to do with preparing the preacher as the sermon. In those times of prayerful reflection, God works on us at least as much as he works on our notes. We need to become malleable, responsive to his Spirit and humble before him and his people. If you want to become a storyteller, it will require a lot of preparation of you as a person. You must embark upon this before you even think about preparing the story. The six suggestions which follow are to get you started.

1. Train your eyes as ears and your ears as eyes

What do I mean by this? Every time you look at something, be it a fast car or a beautiful sunset, try to think how you might describe it. With the fast car, for example, you might use images from nature, such as a cheetah or a panther. Equally, with the sunset you might turn to the world of art – talking about Turner's palette, perhaps, or music – talking of deep mellow notes. You can then do the same in reverse with sounds. If you hear a pneumatic drill somewhere nearby splitting up the road – what visual images could you use to describe the sound to someone who had not heard it? As you hear waves break over a breakwater – what visual images could you use to describe it to someone over the phone? This deliberate crossing over of the aural and visual helps you to master the art of description. When it comes to telling your story, you will have to stimulate the senses of your listeners through words alone – so it is as well to practise first in the privacy of your own mind. The good thing about this is that you can practise it anywhere at any time. Try it today.

2. Train your mouth as a paintbrush

Now that you have learnt to look at sounds and listen to sights, try taking it a step further. Think of the silence before you as an empty canvas. How can you paint a picture onto it with words? Think back to that sunset. How can you describe it in such a way now that a picture is created in the minds of those who listen? Again, it is best to start this in the privacy of your own mind before trying it out on others. Watch the sun set tonight and write a description of it. Put the description of it away until tomorrow evening, and then read it again. Does it evoke the scene for you? If not, keep trying it until it does. As you practise this, make sure you listen to the radio as often as possible. Listen especially to news correspondents, capturing the scene before their eyes without pictures to help them. You will find Jolyon Mitchell's review of creative speech in radio broadcasting, *Visually Speaking*, especially helpful here.

3. Read short stories

Obviously, it is good for you as a communicator to read almost anything – newspapers, novels, devotional books … or even comics! However, the short story is of particular help when it comes to preparing sermons. Unless you are intending to keep your congregation rooted to the spot for hours on end, the short story will meet your needs more exactly. It will show you the discipline involved in developing an intriguing plot and believable characters in a short space of time. Look at how the author has constructed the whole thing to draw you into the story at the start and to touch you by the end. Were you left puzzled, amused, angry or just downright intrigued? Whichever it was – how did the author make you feel it? Pay particular attention to the use of description.

4. Watch adverts

Okay, so perhaps you do despise them with their cheery jingles, their infuriating voice-overs and their zany graphics. That said, I'm sure you remember them! Advertisements are often the epitome of efficient and creative communication. Especially where television adverts are concerned, vast sums of money have been paid for a few precious seconds of airtime in order to sell their product. How have they done it? What do you notice about the images and the words? How is the producer's creativity expressed? Even if you never buy the product, you can learn from the process. Not only that, but it also means that you can redeem the time spent watching them, in the truest sense of the word!

5. Observe stand-up comics

Nowadays, it is hard to find a stand-up comic to observe where at least part of their routine won't make your toes curl with embarrassment. However, as a putative storyteller, they have a great deal to teach you. These people have to hold a sceptical audience for anything up to an hour with only their words to help them. At least your congregation are unlikely to boo you off the stage or pelt you with beer glasses. That said, look at the way the comic holds his or her audience. Look at the way their keen observation of life has allowed them to describe people we all recognise. Listen to the way they use words … and pauses to hold our attention, building up to a comic climax or punchline. As is often said, the secret of good comedy is timing – but it can do a lot for the storyteller too!

6. Look at everything more intently

From now on, don't just look at things with your eyes – look at them with your mind, and even your soul. Don't just think to yourself 'that grass is green' – what kind of green is it? Is it light green or dark green, acid green or restful green? I have been helped greatly in this by taking up watercolour painting and spending many years in the pursuit of authentic trees and believable seas! However, you don't need to go to those lengths in order to see things more intensely.

We can learn here from two very different walks of life. Many nuns are taught the discipline of *devotio* from their earliest days. *Devotio* is the practice of devoting yourself utterly to whatever you are doing at a given moment, without allowing your mind to be distracted by other things. Thus, for instance, a nun practising *devotio* properly will be thinking only about sweeping while she sweeps the yard. Her whole being is devoted at that moment to making the yard as clean as it can possibly be for the glory of God. Other things, even overtly holy things, can wait until later.

When you are looking at the scene before you, be it a tiny ladybird crawling across a leaf or a vast storm-cloud unfurling across the sky – try to give your all to looking at it. Other things can wait for a moment. In this way, you will experience the scene at the maximum intensity, which will help you to describe it (or other scenes like it) later.

The other piece of advice comes from an old wood-carver. He was teaching a young boy how to carve beautiful wooden animals, and this is the advice he gave. He told him to take one of the animals and to squeeze it tightly, tightly in his own hand. In fact, he was to squeeze it as tightly as he possibly could without hurting himself, to the point where its impression was left on his palm. After that, with the impression still there, he was to take chisel and wood and fashion his own masterpiece. Starting with the world around us, we need to start experiencing things with that kind of intensity. Once we have done so with the world we see, we can then take the next leap and begin to do so with the stories we find in the Bible.

Preparing the story

As you get more used to preparing the kind of narratives we have seen in Chapters 4–6, much of what follows will come naturally to you. However, it is good to observe the following disciplines anyway, since they help with the construction of a well-rounded narrative.

1. Ensure that the Bible passage is read as well

For us as preachers, this is of the utmost importance. No matter how skilful we may be at storytelling, nor how many hours we have spent labouring over the narrative we deliver, we still believe the Bible to be the inspired Word of God. If the only version of a story which is heard is our own retelling of the Bible, then we run the risk of depriving our hungry congregations of a square meal! We want people to retain not only our retelling of the story, but the actual Bible story too. One way to ensure that they do both is to read the passage as close to the sermon as possible, preferably with no music or other interlude between.

2. Check your facts

As has been mentioned in previous chapters, there is a wealth of reference material available for use in sermon-preparation. Between printed material and information available online, it is possible to find out even the smallest of details about life in Bible times, from the clothes people wore to the seeds they sowed. It is incumbent upon you as the preacher to find out any of these facts which are germane to the narrative before you write it. In this way, you can avoid any unnecessary anachronisms which might prevent listeners from taking the sermon seriously. It should be noted, however, that incidental details are only that – incidental. If we allow our message to stand on the fragile basis of an incidental detail which we have added into the story, then it is likely to topple over.

3. Use all five senses

Once again, this is a point to which we have already alluded. Having written your narrative, read it through again and see if you have incorporated all five senses. This is important because it brings the story to life, and it also maximises its impact among the listeners. Although it may seem contrived to you, it will be vital to someone who is listening.

4. Major on your minor ones

We all have a natural inclination towards either visual or audio clues in our speech pattern. Thus, some people will say 'I hear what you are saying' while others will say 'I see what you mean'. Both of them mean the same thing, but their choice of language reveals their particular inclination. Which expression would you be more likely to use? Whichever it is, you need to insert a positive bias in the opposite direction in your storytelling. In so doing, you will offset your natural tendency and finish up with a well-balanced narrative.

5. Use silence

Silence in speech, like white space on a printed page, is vital in order to get the message across. An unrelenting piece of text with no gaps whatsoever is harsh on the eye, and ends up discouraging the reader from continuing. Conversely, a little white space here and there serves only to emphasise the words which *are* written, making them stand out. In the same way, silence in storytelling can serve to heighten the drama of the story as it unfolds. It also acts as an excellent prelude to the moment of revelation or application. You will need to steel yourself to use it, though. It is an established fact that thirty seconds of silence to the congregation feels like at least ten minutes to the preacher who has created it! Persist, though, and you will find that it pays dividends.

Exercises in creativity

1. Ready to hand

Pick up an object now. It might be something you have in your pocket or your handbag as you read this book on a train. Alternatively, it might be something on the desk in front of you. As you turn the object over in your hands now, ask yourself some questions about it. Where did it come from? You might answer this by turning it over and looking underneath, or simply by remembering the occasion on which it was bought. Next, ask yourself how it came to be where it is now. Is it because you forgot to put it away in its proper place, or is it there in your hand now for a particular reason? Perhaps it was given to you as a thank-you, or a keepsake, or even a warning! After you have answered those questions, pick a point in the distant future, perhaps three to five years away, and speculate on where the object might be then. Perhaps it will still be in your handbag because that's where it belongs. Alternatively, both the object and the desk on which it sits might be swept away by an earthquake or a flood. Then again, perhaps you will throw it away, and then where will it go? Before you know where you are, you are off on a narrative journey with this chance object ...

2. Try out a kenning

A kenning is an Anglo-Saxon literary device whereby a new noun or noun-phrase is used to replace a more familiar noun. Thus, the noun 'mother' might be replaced by 'child-raiser', or the word 'brother' by 'cot-shaker'. The possibilities are endless! Once we start on Biblical words, we really begin to stretch our imagination. Thus, a prophet might be a 'hope-breather' or a priest a 'God-whisperer'. By thinking up these kennings, it makes you think about the qualities of the person or the role you are describing, and pushes you outside the familiar into more creative use of language. Start off by finding kennings for the following list, and then add some more of your own:

Adam, Moses, psalmist, king, disciple, apostle, missionary, angel.

3. Write a travel diary

Next time you go on holiday, whether somewhere exotic or familiar, keep a diary of your experiences. Try to avoid the barely factual such as 'went to beach', and opt instead for the descriptive: 'the beach was like a moving carpet of humanity today – a tapestry of other people's towels'. You need not show this diary to anyone else (unless you really want to), but by keeping it you will begin to develop creative skills in recording even the most ordinary experiences. You might even enjoy it!

4. The creative challenge

Now that you are really ready to put pen to paper and write a Biblical narrative, stop! Before you write any words, see if you can do it in pictures first. Take your narrative, and see if you can express it either in a collage of images torn from magazines and catalogues, or in a simple storyboard format. The storyboard might consist of six or seven (very rough) sketches of what happens as the story progresses. The purpose of this is to ensure that the limits of your creativity are not limited by words alone. In other words, it ensures that your understanding of the story and its life is not defined purely by your vocabulary. This can be a great way to 'get into' the story, and not just for you as preacher. Try getting a small group to do it with the story of Jonah and the whale or Jesus and the ten lepers, for instance. The results can be both hilarious and revealing! This exercise will help you to summarise what you really want to say about the story before the difficult business of choosing words actually begins.

A whole Bible lies before you just waiting to be preached. In your mind, you have all sorts of techniques which have heightened your awareness both of the Bible and of the world to which it speaks. Sunday is heading towards you with all the certainty of an oncoming express train, and you just can't wait to try these new techniques out. However, before you do, there are some steps to consider when it comes to introducing it in your particular context. It is to those steps that we now turn.

Chapter 8

The way ahead

When I first heard about narrative preaching, I approached it with a peculiarly British degree of scepticism. My hackles instantly rose against the speakers and writers who appeared to have a Messiah complex about this new technique. They seemed to have undergone a transformation from 'ordinary preacher' to 'narrative preacher' overnight, and I was less than convinced. However, it did not take me long to realise that, behind the overwhelming enthusiasm, a very serious point was being made. Their argument, based on scripture, psychology and experience, was that stories really work in the preaching environment. Because of their ability to tap into the deepest veins of our longings and desires, these stories are a powerful weapon in the preacher's armoury. After just one week, I was convinced, and very keen to try it out. At a prayer meeting with some of my colleagues, I described myself as feeling like a child with a new toy on his lap – anxious for the journey home to be over so that I could unwrap it and play with it straight away. While you may not describe your own feelings in quite that way, perhaps you too are keen to try out this special style of preaching. Not surprisingly, I would encourage you wholeheartedly to do so. However, before embarking on this storytelling adventure, there are one or two cautionary notes to sound.

Check your motives

This is the point at which, along with the psalmist, we should ask God to 'search me and know my heart' (Psalm 139:23). As preachers, we always want to communicate the Word of God in the best and most effective way to those who listen. In this process, we wring our hearts, wrestle in our minds, and burn up our very souls on the altar of getting the message across. At the moment we stand up to preach, nothing matters more than proclaiming the Word of God. At that moment, we want nothing more than to be certain that the Word is heard. That said, we are also prey to the same kind of vanity which troubles many in positions of influence. We want to please people, and we want them to be pleased with us. Not only that, but also if we can impress them with our knowledge and skill along the way and leave them longing to hear more from us in future – then we are happy.

From time to time, these mixed motives are inevitable. They will continue to be a problem until the day we are perfected in the presence of God. However, until that day comes, we need to keep them in check. Ask yourself right now: what are my motives for wanting to try out narrative preaching? If you feel that your preaching has become stale and you want to refresh it – carry on! If you feel that attention levels in your congregation have been flagging and this might be a way to revive them – go right ahead! If you want to wow them with your new-found gifts and reduce them to tears in the aisles, it might be wise to pause. In quietness and reflection, allow God to remind you again of his call to preach. You are, at most, the messenger. If at the end of the sermon the thing people remember most is how you delivered it, then their focus (and probably yours) has been all wrong. Once you are sure of your motives, it is time to proceed.

Know your flock

How well do you know your congregation? Ideally, you should know the kinds of newspapers or books they read, the sort of programmes they watch on television and the kind of films they are likely to watch at the cinema. This is not because it is your job to police them, or in any way to pass judgement on those choices. However, since it is your job to communicate with them, you need as clear an idea as possible about what makes them tick. This will enable you to streamline the communication process by 'speaking their language'. That language may be specific to a given town or village, or even to a specific church within that village. Over the years, particular words will have acquired particular meanings among this group of people. Even words in common parlance elsewhere will have a particular resonance for these people on account of their shared history and experiences.

The story is told of a new primary-school teacher who arrived to teach a Reception class in a village school in Devon. Most of the children were from farming families and travelled into the school from the outlying farms. As she progressed with the children through the alphabet, she reached the letter P. Holding up a big coloured picture of a pig, she asked what it was. The children stared back at her with puzzled faces, growing more anxious as her questioning became more intense. Finally, one brave little boy put his hand up tentatively. 'Yes,' she gasped, relieved, 'what is it?' 'Please, miss,' the little boy replied, 'is it a one-year-old Gloucester Old Spot?' Local 'flavour' has a big impact on communication!

This kind of inside information will be invaluable to you when it comes to choosing both the kind of narrative you preach and the kind of vocabulary you use. In some contexts, richly descriptive second-voice narratives will be greatly appreciated, while in others the immediacy of a first-voice narrative will go down far better. Equally, in some places, images taken from art and literature can be usefully woven into your narrative, whereas in others cinematic allusions will have far more impact. Before you go any further, sit down now and write down all you know about the language of your congregation. You probably know more than you realise!

Anticipate the difficulties

Because narrative preaching is new to many, it is unlikely to receive an unquestioning acceptance in your congregation. Even if they have accepted stories as illustrations in the past, they are likely to baulk when you first start to use stories as the key vehicle for truth in your sermons. You should not be put off by this, since you have come to the conviction that this technique has much to offer. However, it is best to anticipate some of the objections in advance.

Just telling stories

Some will feel that, instead of really preaching, you are 'just' telling stories. Although you have researched the background carefully and brought your Biblical scholarship to bear in the crafting of the narrative, this is not necessarily obvious in the finished product. Indeed, if your narrative is crafted carefully enough, it *should not* be. However, since stories are often the lighter moments of illustration within the traditional sermon, some will struggle to believe that a story can bear the full weight of the sermon's meaning. On the first occasion I ever preached a narrative sermon, one listener asked afterwards: 'was that it – aren't we getting a sermon tonight?' Bear in mind that the people who feel this most strongly are likely to be those whose view of the sermon's importance is very high. This means that their aims are actually the same as yours.

Entertaining, not educating

With some people, the moment you use the word 'story', it suggest something fictitious and even frivolous. If it does have any continuing importance, it is only in their subconscious. The effortless simplicity of learning through stories which happened in their early years has been overlaid with adult learning and bookish wisdom. They dismiss them as useful only for entertainment, for children, or for those in primitive rural communities. Even those well versed in the Bible stories of Jesus would be at best surprised and at worst dismayed to find their preachers employing the same storytelling techniques. Many would dismiss it as childish and inappropriate. After all, the only people who tell stories to adults in public tend to be stand-up comedians who do so in order to raise a laugh. Even though it will soon become obvious that you are not looking for laughs, the narrative approach nonetheless engages the emotions and the senses far more than other styles. Those who expect the preacher to teach them will find this hard to accept. They may believe that you have changed your view of preaching and that you no longer see it as a serious undertaking. If you want to keep them on board, you will quickly need to reassure them on this point.

Selling the congregation short

By their very nature, narrative sermons tend to be shorter than propositional or thematic ones. Much of this is to do with the kind of language being used. Narratives use a condensed form of language, in much the same way as poetry uses language in a more condensed way than prose. A poet will choose two or three words to evoke a particular mood, which might require a paragraph or more in prose. In certain traditions, of course, the shorter the sermon the better. However, if your particular church has been accustomed to forty-five-minute expositions, then a ten-minute narrative is going to come as a rude shock to the system. Your congregation may well feel that you have sold them short. While it is worth bearing in mind that some forty-five-minute preachers stop preaching after twenty minutes and simply carry on speaking, this is not always the case. The value of the short narrative sermon will have to be proved on the depth of its impact.

The other way in which they may feel sold short is that some narrative sermons, as we have seen, leave the application to the listeners. Instead of concluding the sermon with a summary of the main thrust, the preacher leaves it with an ambiguous ending. Some will respond very positively to this kind of challenge, but others will simply feel that you have been too lazy to finish the sermon off properly. Only explanation … and fruit will prove them wrong.

Prepare the ground

If you are now at the point that you would like to try narrative preaching, it is because you have been persuaded of its worth. After looking again at the value of preaching, you have considered the changing linguistic landscape and the need for lyrical language in the pulpit. After that, you have carefully examined three different kinds of narrative preaching, assessing their particular strengths and weaknesses before deciding to try it out for yourself. Bear in mind that your congregation has not been privy to any of the above. As far as they are concerned, they are expecting you to preach next Sunday in just the same way as you have always done – whatever that might be.

You need to find a way of communicating not just where you have arrived in your feelings about the place of narrative in preaching, but also how you got there. What made you feel that prosaic and propositional preaching was not the only way? Equally, what made you feel that narrative preaching had something to offer? If you have come prayerfully to these convictions, you should have no hesitation about sharing them. There are a number of ways to do this. It might be that you take a slot in the service, apart from the preaching, to talk about the different style you will be adopting on this occasion. You may choose to do it even more carefully and to talk *this* week about the style you will be trying out *next* week. The main thing to get across is that this is not novelty for novelty's sake, but that you want God's Word to come across in the most powerful and direct way possible. Reassure people that you will not be preaching like this all the time from now on, but that you believe it is an approach worth taking with certain passages on certain occasions.

It may also be worth encouraging others to join you on the journey. Why not set some home-group studies on Bible stories using the preparatory techniques outlined in Chapters 4–6? In this way, people will see for themselves the possibilities and the challenge of plunging into the Biblical story. My own experience has been that encouraging groups to interact with Bible stories in this way can produce moments of great hilarity and searing insight. It was on just such an occasion, after retelling the story of Jonah, the rebuked jingoistic prophet, that one home-group member commented on how much he sounded like a tabloid-reader! That person went away understanding Jonah's personality and God's dealings with him in a way that he had never done before.

Check the response

The word 'feedback' is liable to strike terror into the hearts of many preachers. It is bad enough facing people's unsolicited criticism without going off to look for it! The preacher who looks for feedback, they feel, is a fool who runs to meet trouble. Of course, there are always times when we feel more acutely vulnerable than others. However, stop and think why you are reading this book. Your heart's desire is to preach well, is it not? And what does preaching well mean? A good preacher is not someone who simply performs well, like a seal at the circus. A good preacher is a man or woman who loves the Word of God and listens to the Spirit of God with such an ardour that they are able to communicate the priorities of heaven to the sons and daughters of earth. If that is what we really want, then it is worth checking to see whether it is happening.

We all know that it is perfectly possible to step down from the pulpit feeling that you have delivered a powerful word, when everybody else thinks you were having an off day (and vice versa). When trying out a new technique, it is more important than ever to check whether it is helping people to hear from God. You might do this in a number of ways, both formal and informal. At the informal end, it is just a case of chatting with one or two trusted people whom you had warned in advance that you would be trying something new. If you wanted to try a more formal approach, either you could bring a 'listening group' together to reflect over several sermons, or you could put some kind of (anonymous) survey round church home-groups. However you do it, the most important thing is that you hear what people have to say. Of course, if you go the selective route, you need to be careful that you don't choose people whose opinions you know in advance, whether negative or positive.

Amend the approach

Many years ago, when I was involved in theatre productions, an experienced actor gave me the following advice: 'in rehearsal, always agree with everything the director says about how to play the scene – then go right ahead and play it the way you always intended to'. If you ask for feedback and then seem entirely unmoved by it, people will soon stop giving it! This does not mean, of course, that you should abandon the narrative experiment entirely if people don't like it; but you may need to amend your approach. If you truly believe that this is the best way to unleash the dynamic power of God's Word, then you need to find a way of pressing ahead with which your particular congregation can be comfortable. In my own church, for example, feedback from trusted church members has led me to favour the third voice over the other styles – although this is counter to my natural inclination. While you are not there to serve people's whims, you are there to meet their spiritual needs. Allow the congregation's response to guide you in how far and how fast you embrace the narrative approach.

Now that the groundwork is laid and the whole enterprise has been trailed, it is time to embark on the adventure of narrative preaching. Let me sound a note of caution, however. If we are truly sensitive preachers, sensitive to the Word, the Spirit and the congregation, then there is no one-size-fits-all sermon type. In Chapter 9, you will find advice on how to select suitable material for narrative preaching – and when to avoid it!

Chapter 9

Proceed with caution

Let's take a moment to scroll back through the centuries to Aristotle, acknowledged by many as the father of rhetoric, in the fourth century BC. In his view, there were three key purposes to communication – namely ETHOS (appealing to the moral being), PATHOS (appealing to the emotional being) and LOGOS (appealing to the rational being). He also recognised three key elements to the act of communication – namely TEXT, WRITER and READER, or TEXT, MESSAGE and AUDIENCE. This is known by many as the 'rhetorical triangle'.

Of course we would want to say that, in the act of preaching, not only do these elements come together, but so does God himself. In Figure 9.2, it is impossible to tell whether God is drawing

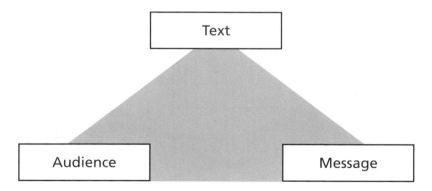

Figure 9.1: The rhetorical triangle

people in through the spiral or sending them out – perhaps both are true. We could say that he communicates the message to the preacher, who then crafts it into the sermon, which then moves the congregation. This would be a centripetal force. Alternatively, we could say that the congregation is drawn into the message, through the agency of the preacher, who is drawn towards God. All the centrifugal force here comes from God himself.

If we were to take those elements of message, speaker, audience and God himself, how do they play in making the decision when we should or should not preach narratively? Where does priority lie in making the decision? In order to answer that difficult question, I believe that there are in fact five elements which we should consider.

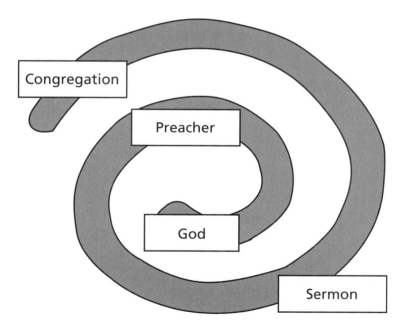

Figure 9.2: The preaching spiral

1. Preacher

The first element is the preacher him- or herself. No-one should feel obliged to undertake narrative preaching, any more than they should feel obliged to adopt a closely expository style. If you have read the descriptions of narrative preaching so far, and find yourself keen to try it out – then do so! If, on the other hand, you are interested by what you read, but don't feel ready to try it out just now, then maybe it is better to wait. You may lack confidence in your vocabulary or in your public-speaking skills which make you hesitant about trying such a new approach. If so, why not try it out in a smaller context such as a home-group or a ministers' fraternal before you take the plunge on a Sunday? However, if you feel that you have the skills and you are raring to go, there are other elements to consider.

2. Passage

No matter how radical our approach, the Bible is and will always remain our primary source material. This means that the first question we must ask about any passage is whether or not it will lend itself to a narrative approach. If it will, then we can bring out the passage's true beauty and depth through this form-sensitive style. If not, then sermon and scripture will end up grating against each other, and no-one will be blessed – least of all the preacher! Not surprisingly, the different genres lend themselves differently to a narrative approach.

Law

The passages in the Pentateuch where the commandments are given and the sacrificial and social laws are spelt out do not provide the best material for a narrative sermon. It is hard to tackle sacrificial laws or descriptions of the tabernacle in any of the three voices we have outlined. That is not to say, however, that it is impossible. Interwoven with the laws, there are small passages of narrative, giving the story of how and where those laws were given, and the initial response to them. These could be used as a route into our feelings about God's laws and their impact on our lives. An alternative is to take a given law, such as the injunction not to covet, and to set it in a modern context, such as inter-neighbour envy.

History

The historical books include those named after an individual (Joshua, Ezra, Nehemiah) as well as those of a more general nature such as 1 and 2 Kings, 1 and 2 Chronicles and 1 and 2 Samuel. In the New Testament, the book of Acts takes up the historical narrative. Not surprisingly, these books provide a rich seam for the narrative preacher. In themselves, they are a communication of truth through story, and therefore give the perfect springboard for narrative preaching. The main danger, however, is to embellish them too much. Some preachers explain a historical story with the retelling of that story, and then go on to layer contemporary stories on top. The result can be bewildering for the listener, and can leave them a long way from the passage where they started. Be warned!

Poetry and wisdom

When it comes to Biblical poetry, I would advise the budding narrative preacher (and all but the most gifted expository preachers) to leave well alone. The only exception to this is those psalms where we are given some background story to their writing, such as Psalm 52. In most modern Bible translations, a short introduction is given in italics at the head of the psalm where the background story is known. Alternatively, it is worth checking one or two Bible commentaries to see what is known of the psalm's 'back story'. Where such a story is known, a reading of the psalm could lead into a narrative sermon on the back story, and then back into the psalm again to finish. The pithy phrases of the wisdom literature do not convert well into narrative sermons. The only way to use them narratively would be, like the laws, to take one or two and transpose them into a contemporary story setting.

Prophecy

There is much narrative material to be found in the prophets, especially the major ones. Often, we are told a lot about the life of the prophet and how they suffer for their calling. Elijah's crisis of confidence after Carmel and Jeremiah's lament in the stocks is just crying out to be preached narratively. Also, Hosea's costly ministry, where even his marriage fell prey to the need to communicate, offers much material for the narrative preacher. The only danger here is that their stories are so absorbing, especially in their darker moments, that the preacher must remain watchful about the need to edify!

Gospels

The Gospels offer perfect material for narrative preaching, both in the parables and in the accounts of Jesus' life and teaching. It is for this reason that there is a strong bias towards them in the samples discussed in Chapters 4–6. The only danger here is that they are among the best-known stories in the world. The preacher must chart a course between the lure of novelty and the strength of familiarity. By all means retell the stories, bringing out the particular burdens which God has given you for your congregation. However, bear in mind that the Gospels themselves have brought many people to Christ – so don't gild the lily too much!

Letters

Although not an obvious source for narrative preaching, in fact the letters have a lot to offer. This is especially the case with the Pastoral Epistles, where Paul writes with a particularly personal flavour and allows certain tantalising clues about his emotional life to slip out. However, even with the general epistles, some careful Biblical background research can put you in touch with the back story of why and when the particular letter was written. This can be especially helpful when preaching a sermon to introduce a series on that letter. A still more creative angle might be to take an issue raised in one of the letters, such as the issue of Christians taking each other to court in 1 Corinthians 6:1–8. This could be set in first-voice narrative as the response of someone hearing the letter read out in church, yet struggling with that issue.

Apocalyptic

In some ways, this is easier with Old Testament apocalyptic than New Testament. At least with Daniel and Ezekiel, we have elements of their life story woven in with the prophetic passages. In this way, we can set the more troubling visions within a narrative context. We can do this with John's revelation when it comes to an introductory sermon setting it in context, though it might be difficult with the more colourful passages.

In the end, you must ask whether the passage you have chosen will best be communicated through a narrative approach. Will one of the narrative voices allow the passage to speak for itself? Will a narrative approach bridge the gap between the then of the passage and the now of the listener in an effective way? If it will, then set to work on crafting a narrative sermon. If not, then be true to your calling as a *servant* of the Word by adopting another approach this time.

3. Theme

Because we inhabit a world of stories, narrative can offer a great way to link an otherwise abstract theme into the realities of daily living. Almost any theme from marital infidelity to fiscal propriety can be explored through story. It is our job as narrative preachers to do that in such a way that the Biblical story brings its full force to bear upon our lives. A well-crafted story can give teeth to a Biblical principle – showing how it impacts on flesh-and-blood human beings. However, I need to sound a cautionary note here about over-layering the stories. Suppose you are in pastoral charge of a local church. That church is overcoming the odds to build something new in the face of opposition without and within. In such a context, you might well choose to preach through the book of Nehemiah. If so, then you already have the story of Nehemiah (known to some) and the story of the Church (known to all) to deal with. To add another layer of invented story would be to confuse matters. In local church ministry, a group of God's people are writing their own story as they tend that corner of the kingdom. Don't overlook the powerful element of communal story in your preaching.

4. Occasion

We have already touched on this in Chapters 4–6. Preaching narratively on a key date in the Church calendar is a high-risk strategy. The kind of dates I am thinking of are Easter Sunday, Christmas services, Pentecost and maybe even harvest. On the one hand, these are the occasions when you are likely to have visitors in the church. What an opportunity to show them that preaching isn't all about soullessly handing down facts from on high. This may be your one opportunity in the whole year to show them that scripture can capture their imaginations. On the other hand, it may be that they come to church on this one occasion precisely because they are seeking the traditional and the familiar. If your approach is too radical and unexpected, they could spend the whole service worrying about that rather than listening to what God is saying. Equally, members of your congregation may feel that these special occasions are opportunities for spelling out the key claims of the Christian faith in the clearest and most unequivocal fashion. In the end, only you as preacher can make the decision. Will you err on the side of caution, or take a risk?

5. Congregation

Your congregation will have particular preferences when it comes to preaching. Numerous factors have contributed to this. They might include spiritual background, education, upbringing and simple taste. When they call you to be their preacher, they call you to work on their behalf. Week after week, they send you into the Word and up the mountain of prayer with the express intent that you should return with an authentic word of God for them. This means that to a certain extent your preferences in preaching style must be governed by theirs. You are there to preach not for your own sake, but for theirs. Imposing a particular style on them just because it suits you would be an abuse of your position.

This does not mean, however, that you must always adhere to the style which has been familiar to them. If this were the case, then they would still be listening to the style of language and sermon which was in vogue fifty or 100 years ago. If you are convinced by the arguments you have read so far that a narrative approach can release the power of God's Word in an authentic way, then it is incumbent on you to try it out no matter what the consequences. You will serve your people better by riding out their discomfort in the short term than bowing to their habits in the long term. Of course, you must adapt the approach in the light of comments received, as suggested in Chapter 8. However, to abandon the narrative experiment entirely may rob them and you of a richer experience of God's Word.

If you have before you now a passage and a theme and an occasion which lend themselves to a narrative approach; if you are willing to try it and you are prepared to pray for your congregation as they sample it – then now is the time to try. In the Appendix, you will find some 'narrative nuggets' to get you started.

Chapter 10

Organic preaching is here to stay

Fad or fabulous?

When I am reading a book like this one, there is usually a question forming in my thoughts by this stage. It rises from the back of my mind to my conscious thought, like an air bubble rising through a glass of liquid. Although I have enjoyed learning about a new style, and although I can feel the author's enthusiasm coming off the page in waves, this is my question: is it just a fad? It was certainly a question I asked when I was first introduced to the narrative preaching style. While its advocates speak of it with a boundless enthusiasm born of experience, does that necessarily mean that it works for the rest of us? Is it not just a matter of personal taste, which in the end will change as it does with every fad?

You won't be surprised to learn that I believe this *is* an enduring tool for the preacher's toolkit, and not just the latest gizmo for the enthusiast. After all, when we look back into the scriptures, we can find the prophets using storytelling as a vehicle for truth millennia ago. Men like Hosea, Amos, Nathan and Ezekiel were acutely aware of the power of story in communicating truth. The people who listened to them were not just touched by their aura or awed by their presence; they were also captivated by their stories. Whether in the royal throne room or the market square, it was often by telling stories that they gained enough attention for God to speak his mind through them.

When the time was right, and the Messiah of God came to the earth, he took on the storyteller's mantle too. Alongside his powerful teaching and his incredible miracles, he demonstrated the art of the parable – the earthly story with a heavenly significance. His ministry is peopled with the characters of good Samaritans and bad Pharisees, kind publicans and anxious widows whom he invented just to get his point across. If a man with miracles at his fingertips and angels at his command felt that stories were important in communicating the Kingdom, we need to have a very good reason for ignoring them!

Not only this, but we can also look outside the Christian Church to see that stories often unlock the creaky doors of hearts and minds. If you delve into the world of personnel-development and change-management, it won't be long before you find somebody telling you about the value of storytelling in communicating vision and motivation. Around the world right now, hard-nosed executives and their advisers are swallowing their pride and recapturing the art of telling stories. Why? Because stories allow both teller and listener to process the really important things at the deepest level. This is to say nothing of the multi-billion-dollar film industry, where stories are crafted with the utmost care so that people in their thousands will pay to be moved by them!

If we want to communicate with the hearts as well as the minds of the people in our churches, then stories are here to stay.

Always and forever?

If stories are so important, does this mean that every sermon from now on must follow a narrative pattern? Certainly not! As I have outlined in Chapter 9, there are some passages, some themes and some occasions which will simply not lend themselves to a narrative approach. If we adopt it unthinkingly, we will actually undermine the Bible instead of releasing its power. Furthermore, the intrigue and the surprise so vital to good narrative preaching will diminish considerably if we use it every week! The preacher who tells every sermon *as* a story is as predictable as the preacher who used to start every expository sermon *with* a funny story. If you preach every sermon as a narrative from now on, then your congregation at least is unlikely to believe that this book was a good investment!

Even if the narrative sermon is not always the right one to preach, do we believe that it will be there forever as one of our preaching tools? If we mean will it be there forever using the style and the images that I have outlined here – no. If we mean will it be there forever drawing on the images and idioms typical to the first decade of the twenty-first century – no. If we mean will it be there forever as a tribute to the great exponents of the narrative preacher's art – no. If, however, we mean will it be there forever as a technique whereby contemporary idiom collides with Biblical truth, sending the sparks flying and illuminating the hearts and faces of God's people – then yes.

Organic preaching is here to stay

The answer to the malaise within preaching (whether experienced by the preacher or by the listener) is not narrative preaching or propositional preaching or dramatic preaching or poetic preaching. The answer is organic preaching – where God, preacher, people, Bible and language are locked in a cycle of growth and change whose end result is good fruit and fragrance.

Stale Bread?

Organic preaching recognises that the soil in which people grow, the linguistic air which they breathe and the shape and style of the preacher may change – but the role of God and the Holy Spirit remain the same.

Consider for a moment Figure 10.1. Like any diagram, it has its limitations; but it helps to explain the process of organic preaching. Those of you with clear memories of schoolbook science will recognise that it is based on the water cycle. We shall look first of all at the 'players' in this cycle, and then at the processes.

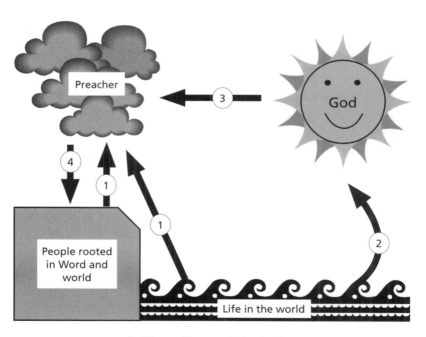

1. Observation   3. Inspiration
2. Prayer   4. Preaching

Figure 10.1: The preaching cycle

Players

People

The people in this cycle are rooted in the world and the Word. They are rooted in the world because they have no choice – by the forces of nature and the providence of God, this is where they were born. They are rooted in the Word because they have chosen it. At a given point, they have decided to accept it as an authentic word from God to humankind. They may vary in their attachment to it, and may interpret its reliability in many different ways. However, they are in the Church and under the ministry of a preacher because they believe that the Bible is, and can be, the Word of God. They approach it each week with a thirst and expectancy born of experience.

Life in the world

Whatever the people hear on a Sunday will wash off them and into their life in the world, like water running off a cliff and into the sea. It will affect their behaviour and their priorities. It will give a distinctive flavour to their life. Sometimes, it will be so diluted as to make scarcely any difference – like the rainwater trickling into the sea. Other times, it will propel them like a torrent into the world which begins on Monday – like an unstoppable river turning salt water fresh. The real test of preaching is to be found more on Monday than on Sunday.

God

God watches over the whole scene, like the sun shining on seas and dry land alike. He hears the prayers rising from his children in the world, he listens to the preacher communicating on his behalf, and he sees the rainfall of his Word as it falls. Without the sun, the cloud cannot rise high enough to rain, and the moisture cannot evaporate from the sea. In the same way, God inspires the preacher while also drawing the prayers out of his people.

Preacher

The preacher sits close to the people, but in close contact with God himself. He or she is moved by the sun, is touched by the moisture from the sea, and gives of her- or himself to the land. The preacher sits on the cusp of land and sea – letting the rain fall on the land but watching to see how it affects the sea. A preacher looks for a Sunday response but longs for a Monday application.

Processes

Observation

The preacher is constantly observing his or her people. This is not in an intrusive way, but in order to understand them and thereby to help them. He or she must observe them both in the church, as they handle the Word, and in the world as they handle their calling. As the cloud draws its moisture from the rivers and streams and also from the sea, so the preacher draws his or her understanding from quiet pastoral observation. If you know lots about how your congregation behave in church, but little about how they behave in the workplace, then your preaching will suffer. Try to devote time not just to studying the Word, but also to studying these precious people whom God has entrusted to you. Your appreciation of them, and of the Word which you seek to apply to them, will grow as you do so.

Prayer

All the way through the week, prayers ascend to God from his people living out their lives in the world. They are praying for his help and looking for strength to live an authentic Christian life in the world. They may also be praying already for next Sunday's sermon – crying out for refreshment as the land might cry out for rain.

Inspiration

Moved by the prayers of the people, and with an eye to the preacher, God provides inspiration. In the water cycle, the sun draws the moisture up from the sea, just as God draws the prayers of his people to himself. In the water cycle, the sun also warms the air, making the cloud rise to the point where it is 'ripe' to release its moisture as rain. God prepares preachers, raising them up and filling them with inspiration, to the point where they have a Word which can refresh and invigorate the people. Preachers often talk about their times of preparation, both during the week and on the Sunday just before the sermon is delivered. However, in truth it is the preacher rather than the sermon which needs to be prepared. As the cloud must reach the right 'texture' to rain, so the preacher must attain the right degree of humility before God and dependence upon God in order to be of any use in the pulpit. More sermons are undone by underprepared hearts than by underprepared notes.

Preaching

Warmed by the sun, saturated with the moisture from streams, rivers and seas, at last the cloud releases its welcome burden. The water pours down on the dry ground, refreshing every place it touches and running off into the waiting waters of the sea. Preaching should come as a release to the preacher and a refreshment to the listener. Sadly, some of the debates about preaching have robbed us of our joy in this anointed task. This is a magnificent calling that we have, and should not be perceived otherwise. In a truly organic model of preaching, the sermon blesses preacher and listener in equal measure.

The hardest thing about describing the preaching process through this model is knowing where to start. Does it start with preaching ... or the praying ... or even the inspiration? Does it start from the preacher, or the people ... or from God himself? Of course, all are true. Like the proverbial chicken and the egg, none came either first or last. What it does show us, however, is the complete interdependence of the different elements. Without sun, evaporation or clouds, no rain falls and nothing grows. In this model, all the 'players' change with the exception of God. Preachers mayhave different forms and styles, just like the different shapes of cloud. Life in the world will inevitably change, just as the levels of the sea rise and fall. People rooted in the world will change, just as the shape of cliffs changes over the centuries. And yet, the process remains the same. To commit to maintaining any single element the same for evermore is a mistake. Rather, we should commit to God and to the process, and pray that the rain will fall!

Organic preachers are committed to a costly, messy relationship with those to whom they preach. They will keep a sharp eye out for any changes in the church environment and the world environment. Where those changes necessitate an adaptation of language or style, they will make it. This is not for the sake of fashion, but rather to ensure that the cycle itself continues. The two immovables in their world are proximity to God and proximity to their people – everything else may change, but they will cling to these until their last breath. This is what organic preaching is all about.

Organic voices

Since we have dwelt so much on different voices in the preceding pages, we shall close with two of them here. Both of them belong to different men of God, and both sound a clear and honest note.

The psalmist in Psalm 137

The most important word for us in this psalm is 'we'. The psalmist is speaking out of a shared situation of misery and longing. Far from home, the psalmist and his people long for happier days. They all but choke when their captors tease them with a demand to strike up a tune from the 'old country'. However, identifying with the people in their sorrow does not mean colluding with them in their defeat. In a supreme effort of faith and will, the psalmist declares that the voice of faith will ring out, and that God's praises will be sung: 'may my tongue cling to the roof of my mouth if I do not remember you, if I do not consider Jerusalem my highest joy' (v. 6). This is a fine example of a truly organic preacher – identifying with people and situation, yet taking them on to new heights of faith and trust.

Ezekiel in Ezekiel 1

Ezekiel's vision of God has to rank as one of the most spectacular and memorable in the whole of the Bible. The prophet himself was so bowled over by it that it left him a quivering wreck face down in the mud, and he had to be specifically bidden by God to stand up and listen. For us, however, it is the context of the vision which is of particular interest. When the vision came, Ezekiel was 'among the exiles by the Kebar River' (v. 1). In other words, this radiant vision of God was experienced in a refugee camp stretched along the muddy banks of the river. Once again, this is a preacher very much in touch with his people. Like them, he is an exile. Like them, he is forced to eke out an existence in these trying circumstances. However, *unlike* them, he is given a vision of God so glorious and beautiful that it restores his belief in the triumph of God's people. A truly organic preacher, Ezekiel lives cheek by jowl with his people – but he also lives close to God. His language is unlike that of any other Old Testament prophet, but his message is the same – God rules, despite the evidence to the contrary.

And so, to preach . . .

As you clutch your hunk of stale bread in your hand, I pray that God has filled you with ideas on how to revive it. I pray, too, that he has taken away your shame about serving up such fare, and given you instead a passion to cook something new. Remember that the things God saw in you when he first called you to preach are still there. Go now and enjoy the stories God has written. Enjoy reading them, and enjoy telling them. As you release the dynamic power of the stories he has written, remember that he is right there beside you.

Remember, too, that words spoken in God's service and under his inspiration can have a far longer life than you expect. In the coldest parts of Siberia, where temperatures can drop to an agonising –60°C, there is a certain time when the air is so cold that your breath freezes as you speak. Referred to by locals as the 'whispering of the stars', this weather means that each word can be heard falling to the ground with a soft 'plop' as it hits the snow. Ancient local legend has it that, come the spring, these words thaw out and can be heard again by anyone who passes by the spot where they were spoken. An inspired storyteller's words have a life far beyond their initial utterance ...

God's best story isn't written yet; he is still working on it. As you embark on the storytelling adventure, you provide him with fresh new material. May each page be better than the last, and may the Storyteller in the end be pleased with the result.

Stale Bread? Refreshing the Preaching Ministry Online

More information and examples of the narrative preaching technique can be found at www.churchofscotland.org.uk/standrewpress

Appendix: Narrative nuggets

Maria Penstone had a point when she wrote that 'God has given us a book full of stories' (in her hymn of the same title; *Baptist Hymnbook*, no. 740). As we have seen, the Bible is filled to the brim with stories, all of which are crying out to be preached. There are the big stories which everyone knows, such as the calming of the storm or the crossing of the Red Sea. Then there are the smaller stories, such as the lesser-known prophets of the Old Testament. On the edges of both these, there are smaller stories still. These are the 'bit parts' in the Biblical epic, the small characters who reflect the enormity of God's plans. Along the way, there are tantalising glimpses of other lives touched by God as he passes – such as the parents of the man born blind in John 9, or the astonished family of the healed demoniac in Mark 5.

In the pages which follow, I have highlighted just thirty of the hundreds of stories which provide material for the narrative preacher. I have already preached on some of them, but most I have yet to tackle. Suggestions are given on the themes they could reflect, and in some cases on the way they could be preached. As soon as you begin to look at them, you may feel a new theme and an entirely different point of view coming to mind. That is a good sign: it proves that you have got the narrative 'itch' already! Before long, you will find that you could double or triple this list of thirty suggestions.

May God bless you as you do so.

Stale Bread?

No.	Description
1	Hagar and Ishmael in the desert, a mother and child on the run. Could be preached in the second voice as the narrator looks at this forlorn scene.
2	Joshua, watching from the sidelines, preparing for greater things.
3	The scene of destruction on the morning after Gideon has destroyed his father's pagan altar. Could be preached in the second voice by a narrator, or in the first voice by one of Gideon's neighbours.
4	Samuel's call, as perceived by Samuel.
5	The widow of Zarephath preparing a last meal for herself and her son, just as Elijah arrives to help them. Would work well in the second voice.
6	Esther risking her life and seeking an audience with the king without permission. Could be preached either in the second voice by a narrator, or in the first voice by Esther herself.
7	Jeremiah's lowest ebb, after a night in the stocks.
8	Nehemiah's midnight journey by donkey around the broken walls of Jerusalem. Could be preached in the first voice by an invented eye-witness.
9	Bravery from the sailors and cowardice from the prophet as Jonah's ship lurches towards Tarshish.
10	Moses on a bluff overlooking the Red Sea, his staff quivering in his hand. Try inventing a first voice for one of Moses' faithful lieutenants, standing close by his side.
11	The arrival of the risen Jesus among the dejected disciples in the locked room.
12	The arrival of the Emmaus disciples with incredible news, only to be told that others know it already!
13	Zaccheus' private session with Jesus. We don't know about the details, only the result. This could be preached powerfully in the first voice by a neighbour of Zaccheus … or even by one of his tax 'victims'.
14	Christ and the woman at the well, noting that she leaves behind the water jar, which was her reason for coming!
15	A boy was brought out of the crowd by Jesus as an example of innocence and trust – what happened to him when he grew up?

Reference	Theme
Genesis 16	Loneliness, God's compassion
Exodus 33:7–11	The importance of preparation in God's service
Judges 6:24–32	Defending your call against every kind of opposition
1 Samuel 3	Obedience to God
1 Kings 17:7–16	God's provision and our faith
Esther 4:1–5:3	Courage
Jeremiah 20	The power of God's abiding presence despite the odds
Nehemiah 2:11–20	Call and vision
Jonah 1	Courage and cowardice before God
Exodus 14:21–8	Belief in God's power despite the crisis
John 20:19–23	Peace in our distress
Luke 24:33–5	Good news upon good news
Luke 19:1–10	The power of Christ's word to invoke change
John 4:1–30	Christ's transforming power
Matthew 18:1–5	Savouring and keeping God's touch

Stale Bread?

No.	Description
16	The slaughter of the innocents. This powerful story needs the raw impact of a first-voice eye-witness.
17	The salvation of the Philippian jailer, with servants and children hauled from their beds to eat a wonderful meal and experience a midnight baptism. Try telling this in the first voice by one of the servants or children baptised that night.
18	Joseph's reconciliation with his brothers, his tears so loud that they could be heard throughout the palace. This touching story requires the second voice.
19	David's moment of revelation from Nathan the prophet.
20	The discovery of the boy Jesus in the temple, told either from his mother's viewpoint or from that of a bystander.
21	The healing of Jairus' daughter, as told by one of the servants sent out of the room.
22	The arrival of the Gadarene demoniac in his home, narrated in the second voice.
23	Paul's initial ministry in Corinth, moved from pillar to post and so down that he needed a specific word from God in order to keep going. This would lend itself well to a third-voice approach, making the bridge from Paul's experience to ours.
24	Jacob's long, anxious night, during which he wrestled with the angel, described in the second voice.
25	The blinding of Saul and his healing by Ananias, as told by one of his entourage.
26	The last supper, especially the washing of the feet and the departure of Judas. Best described in the second voice.
27	Two prophets lose their way. A third voice would allow you to describe the story *and* apply it to our acts of obedience today.
28	Hosea redeems Gomer in the marketplace. This would be very powerful in the first voice, described by an onlooker in the marketplace.
29	A brave servant girl speaks up to heal her master.
30	From blindness, to elation, to rejection, to worship – the story of the man born blind. Second voice is the obvious approach, although it would be very powerful in the first voice from the point of view of the man himself.

Reference	Theme
Matthew 2:13–18	The beauty of Christ against the ugliness of sin
Acts 16:25–34	Excitement at the work of God
Genesis 45:1–15	Reconciliation
2 Samuel 12:1–13	Repentance, the power of the prophetic word
Luke 2:41–51	Coming to terms with the true power and authority of Jesus
Mark 5:35–43	Power of God
Mark 5:18–20	The importance of personal testimony
Acts 18:1–11	Discouragement and faith
Genesis 32	Coming to terms with our past and our future
Acts 9:1–19	The power of God to change a stubborn heart
John 13:1–30	The depth of Christ's humility and love
1 Kings 13	The dangers of distraction from serving God
Hosea 3	The cost of God's redeeming love
2 Kings 5:1–5	Courage against the odds
John 9	The rocky journey of faith

Glossary

Exegesis   The process of digging out the authentic meaning of a Biblical passage through prayer, reflection and research.

Exposition   An explanation of the text, designed to bring out its meaning in the original context and apply it to the contemporary setting.

Form-sensitive preaching   A style of preaching which mirrors the style of the sermon with the style of the text. For example, a Pauline argument is preached in an argumentative style, and wisdom literature in a reflective style.

Hermeneutical   Hermeneutics is the science of textual interpretation in general, and Biblical interpretation in particular. Hermeneutical decisions are those taken by the preacher about how he or she understands the Biblical text.

Homiletical   Homiletics is the science of communication through preaching. Homiletical decisions are guided by the preacher's knowledge of congregation and occasion.

Narrative (first voice)   A narrative told in the first person, whether that person is the key character or an eye-witness.

Narrative (second voice)   A narrative told by a person not directly involved in the story, but acting as narrator.

Narrative (third voice)   A narrative where the first or second-voice technique is combined with comments addressed directly to the congregation by the preacher. In such comments, the narrative will be explained and applied.

Oratory   The classical discipline of informing and persuading through speech.

Organic   The organic model of preaching recognises that preacher, people and context are inextricably linked in the providence of God. It recognises that many of the elements will change, but the growth imperative remains.

Pneumatic   That which is inspired or driven by the Holy Spirit.

Polyvalence   A word, phrase or story with many possible meanings.

Propositional   The style of preaching which consists of presenting theological truths, or propositions, to the congregation.

Bibliography

Alter, Robert, *The Art of Biblical Narrative* (New York: Basic Books, 1981).

Bettelheim, Bruno, *The Uses of Enchantment* (London: Penguin, 1976).

Brueggemann, Walter, *Finally Comes the Poet: Daring Speech for Proclamation* (Minneapolis, MN: Fortress Press, 1989).

Brueggemann, Walter, *The Bible and Post-modern Imagination: Texts under Negotiation* (London: SCM Press, 1993).

Brueggemann, Walter, *Texts that Linger, Words that Explode* (Minneapolis, MN: Fortress Press, 1999).

Cooling, Margaret, *Creating a Learning Church* (Oxford: Bible Reading Fellowship, 2005).

Craddock, Fred, *Preaching* (Nashville, TN: Abingdon Press, 1985).

Craddock, Fred, *As One Without Authority* (St Louis, MO: Chalice Press, 2001 edn).

Day, David, *Embodying the Word: A Preacher's Guide* (London: SPCK, 2005).

Freedland, Jonathan, *Jacob's Gift* (Edinburgh: Hamish Hamilton, 2005).

Grant, Tony (ed.), *From Our Own Correspondent* (London: Profile Books, 2005).

Graves, Mike, *The Sermon as Symphony* (Valley Forge, PA: Judson Press, 1997).

Stale Bread?

Graves, Mike (ed.), *What's the Matter with Preaching Today?* (Louisville, KY: Westminster John Knox Press, 2004).

Jones, Kirk Byron, *The Jazz of Preaching* (Nashville, TN: Abingdon Press, 2004).

Lacey, Rob, *Are We Getting Through?* (Reading: Silver Fish Publications, 1999).

Long, Thomas G., *Preaching and the Literary Forms of the Bible* (Philadelphia, PA: Fortress Press, 1989).

Long, Thomas G., *The Witness of Preaching* (Louisville, KY: Westminster/John Knox Press, 1989).

Lowry, Eugene, *The Homiletical Plot* (Atlanta, GA: John Knox Press, 1978).

McKee, Robert, *Story: Substance Structure, Style and the Principles of Screenwriting* (London: Methuen, 1998).

McKee, Robert, 'Storytelling that moves people', *Harvard Business Review* (June 2003), pp. 5–8.

Marguerat, Daniel and Yvan Bourquin, *How to Read Bible Stories* (London: SCM Press, 1999).

Miller, Calvin, *Spirit, Sword and Story* (Grand Rapids, MI: Baker Books, 1996).

Miller, Calvin, *The Sermon Maker* (Grand Rapids, MI: Zondervan, 2002).

Mitchell, Jolyon, *Visually Speaking* (Louisville, KY: Westminster John Knox Press, 1999).

Payne, Tony, 'An editor's guide to sermons', *The Briefing* (August 2005), pp. 17–18.

Pollerman, Sandra, *Stories, Stories Everywhere* (Oxford: Bible Reading Fellowship, 2001).

Quicke, Michael, *360-degree Preaching* (Grand Rapids, MI: Baker Academic, 2003).

Rose, Lucy Atkinson, *Sharing the Word: Preaching in the Roundtable Church* (Louisville, KY: Westminster John Knox Press, 1997).

Schlafer, David, *Playing with Fire: Preaching Work as Kindling Art* (Minneapolis, MN: Cowley, 2004).

Shah, Selina and Keith Patrick, 'Have you heard the one about?', *CILIP Journal* (October 2002), pp. 40–1.

Standing, Roger, *Finding the Plot: Preaching in Narrative Style* (Milton Keynes: Paternoster, 2004).

Tisdale, Leonora Tubbs, *Preaching as Local Theology and Folk Art* (Minneapolis, MN: Fortress Press, 1997).

Troeger, Thomas, *Imagining a Sermon* (Nashville, TN: Abingdon Press, 1990).

Willimon, William, *Peculiar Speech: Preaching to the Baptized* (Grand Rapids, MI: Eerdmans, 1992).

Webliography

Delin, Melissa, *The Power of Leadership Storytelling*: www.mln.org.uk

Fryer, Bronwyn, *Happy Tales: The CEO as Storyteller*: www.hbswk.hbs.edu

Kinni, Theodore, *Loosen up Your Communication Style*: www.hbswk.hbs.edu

Shepherd, William H. Jnr, *A Second Look at Inductive Preaching*: www.religion-online.org

Simmons, A., *The Six Stories You Need to Know How to Tell*: www.storytellingcenter.com

A Partial Chronology of Organizational Storytelling: www.creating
    the21stcentury.org
Storytelling: A Prime Method of Persuading: www.management
    futures.co.uk

Various resources on global storytelling: www.story4all.com

Acknowledgements

1. Quote from Craig Barnes (p. 4) used with permission of Christianity Today International, Carol Stream, Illinois, USA.
2. Chrysostom quote (p. 19) used by permission of St Vladimir's Seminary, 575 Scarsdale Road, Crestwood, NY 10707. www.svspress.org
3. Frederick Buechner, *Telling the Truth*. © 1977 by Frederick Buechner. Reprinted by permission of HarperCollins Publishers.
4. Page 39: © Walter Brueggemann, *Finally Comes the Poet: Daring Speeches for Proclamation* (Fortress Press, 1989).
5. Kate Adie quote (p. 45) used with permission of Profile Books (2007): *From Our Own Correspondent*.
6. Jonathan Freedland quote (p. 195) by permission of Penguin Group UK.